The Seventh and Final Volume
in the Hull Legacy Series

CONSERVATISM
AND LIBERALISM
IN THE
CHRISTIAN FAITH

Toward a
Moderate Approach

WILLIAM E. HULL

© 2015

Published in the United States by Nurturing Faith Inc., Macon GA,
www.nurturingfaith.net.

Library of Congress Cataloging-in-Publication Data is available.

ISBN 978-1-938514-84-5

Hull Legacy Series

Sponsored by
THE HULL LEGACY SERIES COMMITTEE
MOUNTAIN BROOK BAPTIST CHURCH
BIRMINGHAM, ALABAMA

Harbingers of Hope:
Claiming God's Promises in Today's World
(2007)

Seminary in Crisis:
The Strategic Response of The Southern Baptist Theological Seminary
to the SBC Controversy
(2010)

Beyond the Barriers: Overcoming Hostility in the Church
(rev. ed., 2012)

The Lord's Prayer: Bringing Heaven and Earth Together
(2013)

The Apostles' Creed: A Baptist Interpretation
(2013)

The Quest for a Good Death: A Christian Guide
(2014)

[Bill Hull] knew more than well enough the trials of a peacemaker standing determinedly between two hostile sides. Standing so, he was "seeking clarity rather than victory," as he believed his faith required him to do. In this last testimony, out of his knowledge and his experience, he accomplished a momentous and greatly needed clarity.

Novelist and poet Wendell Berry,
in a letter to David Hull

Bill Hull possessed one of the brightest and keenest minds among Baptists of his generation. Through his preaching, teaching, and writing he demonstrated a special gift of bringing wisdom, clarity, and challenge to difficult and significant issues. He was a consummate theological middleman, bridging the unique domains of the academy and the church. In this his last book, written in the final days of battling a debilitating terminal illness, he pushes the reader toward reconciling two polarities that seem irredeemably opposed and ultimately incompatible. For Christians weary of the culture wars and repulsed by the ugliness of partisan politics, *Conservatism and Liberalism in the Christian Faith* is a helpful guide. Bill Hull leaves the legacy of a generous book that is creative, redemptive, honest, and hopeful.

J. Bradley Creed, President
Campbell University
Buies Creek, North Carolina

William E. Hull's work, *Conservatism and Liberalism in the Christian Faith*, warns us against falling into the trap of "false choices" by looking for ways to build bridges between seemingly opposing viewpoints. Hull shows us how a truly Christian compromise doesn't violate anyone's integrity, but offers instead a path toward reconciliation that raises the possibility of a future forged in cooperation and mutual beneficence, both hallmarks of the historic Baptist witness and one with which Mountain Brook Baptist Church is so pleased to be a part.

Doug Dortch, Senior Minister
Mountain Brook Baptist Church
Birmingham, Alabama

The rare combination of gifts and commitments I found in Bill Hull form the lasting portrait of a scholar and pastor whom the late John Claypool called "the hardest working man I've ever known." It will be no surprise to anyone who knew him, then, that Bill finished this last book even while working through the tortured paroxysms of ALS, which systematically took his voice and his motor skills—though even the tentacles of death were no match for Bill's scholarship and Christian conviction.

Few honest academics have shared Bill's pastoral passion for church and congregation, and fewer pastors have even begun to grasp the broad range of disciplines he had mastered. Bill exercised these dual passions in a time of schism that ruptured his beloved denomination, left and right, and that continues to threaten the nation at large.

It is appropriate, then, that a thoroughgoing dissection and analysis of our bifurcated conscience is the focus of this, his final gift of scholarship. And his most generous contribution, a lasting tribute to his legacy, is his unique, visionary capacity to see a path of harmony and synthesis for church and state, so beautifully endowed is humanity with God's generous diversity.

Bill Hull embodied the right and righteous desire of the conservative: making the collective wisdom of a lived tradition the foundation of our present, while simultaneously embodying the spirit of the liberal: marching fearlessly into an unknown future, clearing new paths, even proclaiming new truths without fear or hesitation. As with everything else Bill Hull taught me, I know I will do well to try to follow his lead.

Russ Dean, Co-pastor
Park Road Baptist Church
Charlotte, North Carolina

Somebody told me in the 1980s, "Bill Hull has a mind big enough to understand all sides of the denominational dispute. He can explain the position of opponents better than they can." He kept on explaining in 2013, even after degenerative disease silenced his speech.

His conversation with God intensified. His mind rose to new heights of perspective. He reached into the depths of his mind to assimilate great knowledge. He laboriously, relentlessly, overflowed his synthesis of life through a fountain pen onto sheets of paper that fell to the floor.

He was a man on divine mission. Awesome! Unforgettable. We can now read the last words of Bill Hull. "God approved of his gifts; Bill being dead yet speaks" (Heb. 11:4). We should read and heed.

Catherine B. Allen, Hull Legacy Committee
Mountain Brook Baptist Church
Birmingham, Alabama

A French philosopher said, "No man is strong unless he bears
within his character antitheses strongly marked.". . . Not ordinarily
do men achieve this balance of opposites. . . . But life at its best is a creative
synthesis of opposites in fruitful harmony. The philosopher Hegel said that
truth is found neither in the thesis nor the antithesis, but in an
emergent synthesis which reconciles the two.

—Martin Luther King, Jr.
Strength to Love

Contents

In Appreciation

This book manuscript is a generous gift to *Baptists Today* news journal
from David W. Hull and Susan Hull Walker, the children of
William E. Hull. Publication and promotion of the book are made
possible through the vision and generosity of the Hull Legacy Series
Committee of Mountain Brook Baptist Church
in Birmingham, Alabama.

Foreword

In *Conservatism and Liberalism in the Christian Faith: Toward a Moderate Approach*, William E. Hull—scholar, educator, pastor, preacher, mentor—provides strategies for understanding and responding to what seem incessant fractures within the Christian church, ideologically represented in our time by the labels "conservative" and "liberal." Hull knew those labels well, not only from his academic research, but also in his own person, particularly in his long association with the Southern Baptist Convention (SBC). Indeed, Hull uses America's largest Protestant denomination (ca. 14 million and declining) as something of a case study for illustrating the larger dynamics of his analysis.

For many, Hull personified those dynamics in himself. Baptist conservatives saw him as the consummate liberal, promoting modernity in his approach to biblical criticism and theological speculation. Yet for many liberals, Hull was the conservative "company man," representing institutional establishments amid accomplished academic rigor. Hence this book, Hull's literal "last words," aimed, he says, at "reconciliation" of issues, ideas, and attitudes that, in his view were present from the church's beginnings, and necessary for its survival!

Before we attribute conservative and liberal approaches solely to the so-called modern or postmodern eras, Hull asks us to recognize their presence in first-century Christianity. Thus Hull identifies certain apostolic "conservatives" such as James who sought to retain various Jewish boundaries for anchoring and informing the fledgling Christian communities. He also explores the approach of apostolic "liberals" such as Stephen and Paul who pushed those boundaries beyond Judaism until the Gentiles "received the gospel." Consequently, he traces the roots of both ideologies from the earliest Christian communities, placing modern conservatism and liberalism within the broader context of longtime biblical, historical, and theological debates and perspectives

Hull's intent is to enlighten in an attempt to reconcile disparate groups within the church, or at least encourage recognition that those disparate approaches to faith, dogma and yes, even gospel, were and remain elements of Christian identity. Using Baptists as one historical example, Hull insists that their radical/liberal response to seventeenth-century religious establishments reflects their conservative attempt to return to an earlier vision of the church, lost, they believed, across centuries of religious establishmentarianism. In his words, for early Baptists, "the only way to conserve the *normative past* was to rebel against the *traditional past*." They broke with the "normative" church of their era "in order to forge a forgotten continuity with the New Testament church." For Hull, Baptist beginnings represented a creative, albeit often chaotic, relationship between certain liberal/conservative insights. I'm still thinking on that.

Likewise, Hull stretches the limits of conservative/liberal outlooks and attitudes in his chapter on theology, exploring topics such as these:

- Eschatology (Is God's New Day then or now?)
- Christology (How might our "unfinished Christological event" define "a distinctive Christian conservatism and liberalism"?)
- Pneumatology ("If the source *never* changes," but "the situation *always* changes," then where is the Spirit moving out ahead of us?)

In this brief book, Hull calls us to account, whatever our ideology of theology and gospel. Churches and schools should find it a valuable introduction to ways of confronting diverse ideas and thought-forms.

And now to full disclosure: I am not terribly objective about Bill Hull and his ideas. Dr. William E. Hull employed me for two of the three legitimate jobs I have ever held as an academic. In 1975, as I was finishing my Ph.D. at Boston University, he hired me, with faculty approval, to teach church history at The Southern Baptist Theological Seminary, Louisville, Kentucky, where he was provost (chief academic officer). I was among the last of his "hires," since in 1975 he departed the seminary to become pastor of First Baptist Church, Shreveport, Louisiana.

Some sixteen years later, he hired me again, this time at Samford University, where he was then provost. By that time I had become identified with the "liberal" element in the SBC, and, as he notes in this study, he was intentional about having me and my more conservative friend, Timothy George, together on the Samford campus. The plan worked, even as Hull received letters praising and/or blaming him for employing one or the other of us. I left Samford after five years to move to Wake Forest University, but his balancing plan continued with other representative conservative/liberal leaning faculty.

At Samford, Bill and I had frequent lunches over which we discussed current events and research interests. He never let me get away with anything, exploring ideas and pressing me on every thesis I proposed— and demanding that I push back. It was great learning and great fun, for both of us, I think. In short, Bill Hull gave me a first and second start: the first when I was a fledgling professor learning the academic ropes, and the second when conservative/liberal conversations turned to diatribe and schism at the very educational institution that offered me a start. He helped me begin and continue, and I am ever grateful.

So this fine work, written with both insight and courage on his way out of this world as a result of ALS, represents Bill Hull's final attempt at reconciliation, or at least recognition that liberal/conservative ideas and ideologies are essential, inescapable, and unending, even in the Church of Jesus Christ. For Hull, they are realities that were present from the church's origins, but they need not (he might say must not) destroy the *Spirit* of Christ that unites us all whether we like it or not. Perhaps in listening to him we will better learn to listen to one another, differing without destroying each other and the Body of Christ.

Bill J. Leonard
James and Marilyn Dunn Professor of Baptist Studies
and Professor of Church History
Wake Forest University, Winston-Salem, North Carolina

Preface

My dad hoped that he would live long enough to finish writing a book about dying. For several years he had been on a journey with ALS (Lou Gehrig's Disease). His book, *The Quest for a Good Death,* was the story of his experience and it offered guidance to others as they faced death. All my life I had learned how to live from my father. In those years following the diagnosis of his terminal disease, I was learning how to die from him as well. He did live long enough to finish the story, even though the book was published after his death.

And then Dad kept on living. . . . After finishing his final book, what would he do next with the remaining months of his life? By this time he could not speak or eat or move anything but his hand and fingers. Yet his mind was still moving, and his spirit was not ready to give up. He kept on writing until he literally could not hold a pen any more. You are holding this last gift to the world.

Why would he continue to write when it had become so physically difficult? Because he had something to say! His grandson and faithful caregiver, Andrew Hull, was there to help—along with a wonderful team of other caregivers. But they could not do the writing for him. Only Bill Hull—the noted scholar, educator, pastor, and Baptist leader—could push through the overwhelming challenges in order to get the insightful thoughts from his head on to the paper for us to read. In his last months this became his mission.

What was so important about writing a book about liberalism and conservatism? With all of the obstacles standing in his way, why not just let this topic be treated by someone else? The answer comes from an interview between my teacher, Dr. Walter "Buddy" Shurden, and my father.

Not too long before my dad experienced the onset of ALS, Dr. Shurden posed twenty questions to him. Dr. Shurden later shared the questions and answers with me, and they were also published as "Bill Hull's Twenty Questions" in *Christian Ethics Today* (Spring 2014, pp. 22-25). Question #14 was provocative: "What is the most important idea in your life? Grace? Calling? Stewardship? As the *Christian Century* once asked. 'What idea has used you?'" Here is how Dad answered the question:

In a word, my controlling idea is Reconciliation. I seek to overcome that polarization by which we keep apart those realities that belong together. Fear and anger almost always lurk where alienation is allowed to flourish. I deplore the ideological rigidity that has rent both our denomination and our country into competing groups. I realize that both ideas and people differ greatly; therefore some type of uniformity is both impossible and undesirable, but I am always striving to achieve balanced complementarity even when it involves holding in tension a great deal of diversity.

Reconciliation was a profound idea that did control Bill Hull. In fact, he spent the last ounces of his energy to share this idea with others. In a day of too much polarization and division, he had an idea that needed to be heard. After a lifetime in ministry that was divided up too starkly with terms such as "liberal" and "conservative," he had an idea that needed to be heard. This book is his effort to "overcome that polarization by which we keep apart those realities that belong together." He truly believed that liberalism and conservatism are "realities that belong together." Now, that is an idea that needs to be heard! Thanks for listening.

David W. Hull

Introduction

I never imagined when I entered the Baptist ministry in 1950 that the categories of conservatism and liberalism would come to dominate and determine the success or failure of my vocation. The terms and their meaning played no part in the churches where I had been raised (1930-1950), nor did they influence the early years of my ministry (1950-1970). I became aware of fundamentalist movements (at Bob Jones University and Tennessee Temple, for example) that used this terminology, but they were on the fringes of Southern Baptist denominational life.

Suddenly, and to many surprisingly, a completely new emphasis arose that contended aggressively and successfully for control of the Southern Baptist Convention (1970-1990). At first, the leaders of this movement used "inerrancy" as their watchword, but, when it proved too complex for grassroots clergy and laity to understand, they shifted to "conservative" and its opposite "liberal"—which had the advantage of already being used by Southerners to explain their sudden shift from the Democratic to the Republican Party. The SBC had long been proud of its unity despite a good bit of intramural conflict, but this polarizing campaign shattered its solidarity for the foreseeable future.

One might suppose that so momentous a schism would call forth a great deal of scholarly study by Baptist intellectuals of the key words "conservative" for the winners and "liberal" for the losers. Instead, the initial literature from both sides of the split was partisan and memoirist, as might be expected from so painful a rupture. Perhaps we are now far enough away from the infighting (1990-2010) to attempt a more objective approach controlled by the canons of established scholarship.

This book is a modest probe in that direction. It seeks to take no side, to interpret only the facts of the subject, and to mediate its underlying scholarship so as to be accessible, not only to Baptist scholars, but also to denominational leaders, pastors, and interested laity. Here, then, is a tract for the times that at least attempts to be serious with a light touch.

An honest word about my own scholarship as reflected by the footnotes: In recent years I have majored on writing books instead of reading them. I could not do both because I have also struggled with the latter stages of a terminal illness, amyotrophic lateral sclerosis. Sad to say, ALS has now done its paralyzing work on my arms and hands so that I can no longer pick up a book or turn its pages. I have been able to provide a brief bibliography of works consulted and to document in the endnotes all instances of direct dependence on a published source. Scholars who note that these citations become sketchy after 1990 and almost non-existent after 2000 are encouraged to fill in the gaps.

Despite these restrictions, I have decided to proceed with publication for two reasons. First, my dialogue here is not with the relevant literature or the scholars who produced it but with the way that the subject is being implemented in Southern Baptist life today.

Second, I have been deeply involved on both sides of the struggle summarized above from its beginning to the present; thus, I felt obligated to share what I have learned both as a participant-observer and as a student of the relevant literature. I leave my readers to judge whether I have been fair to all of the available evidence.

It is a pleasure to acknowledge my first serious treatment of this subject in the Deere Lectures delivered at the Golden Gate Baptist Theological Seminary in 1983. Revised portions of that presentation are embedded in the present work.

William E. Hull

CHAPTER 1

The Irony of the Conservative-Liberal Debate

On November 12, 1982, the recently elected president of the Southern Baptist Convention convened an earnest effort at denominational summitry. For more than three years (1979-1982), the SBC had been embroiled in its fiercest theological controversy since the mid-1920s. Entering office by a narrow margin at a badly polarized convention, the new leader pledged to work for harmony with all factions and immediately set about to fulfill that promise by attempting reconciliation through face-to-face dialogue.

After a preliminary meeting with a few key planners on October 5, 1982, invitations went out to every leader prominently identified with any side of the conflict, most of whom (forty-five) agreed to attend. Never before in this generation had so many prime movers of theological debate among Baptists gathered around the same conference table to thrash out their differences. After spending the morning hearing and responding to a series of position papers, the group settled into serious discussion during the afternoon that reached its emotional climax when one of the participants stood and addressed the chair to this effect:

> Mr. President, you were elected by one group within our Baptist life while I speak now for those in this room and beyond who are identified with another group. The importance of the SBC presidency lies in its appointive power to name certain key committees. Therefore, the "bottom line" of this meeting is whether persons of my persuasion will be given a fair share of your presidential appointments. The key issue is not whether we learn to speak the same theological language today, but whether we shall all feel equally welcome to participate in the same denomination during your tenure.

The moderator had been asked such a question many times before and seemed eager to answer it once again. The style of his response reflected a studied effort to find a formula that would be true to his own convictions and yet not be divisive within the larger constituency. In effect he replied: "I intend to appoint Southern Baptists of demonstrated loyalty and proven experience who are known to be conservative." By inference he just as clearly implied, "I do not intend to appoint Baptists of demonstrated loyalty and proven experience who are thought to be liberal."[1]

The most significant thing about that reply was that "conservatism" versus "liberalism" had become the watershed issue in the formulation of presidential policy. The position taken simply assumed as axiomatic that Southern Baptists are a conservative denomination, hence those who share that viewpoint should be appointed to leadership positions, while those who espouse a liberal outlook should not.

I

I have selected this incident from many that might have been chosen in order to illustrate the most pervasive theological trend of our time: the tendency to absolutize conservatism and liberalism as normative categories for understanding Christian identity. Anyone familiar with Southern Baptist life will know that these terms now dominate all internal theological discussion. Indeed, many use the labels to describe the decisive issue that is sure to determine the ultimate destiny of the denomination; that is, Southern Baptists will rise or fall on whether they are conservative or liberal. Ministers, in particular, are using these same code words to describe themselves both theologically and professionally. Subtle qualifiers seem to say it all: To claim "I am *strongly conservative*" or "I am *moderately conservative*" implies not only what one believes, but also how one preaches and administers and evangelizes. No facet of church life is exempt from being described and evaluated by these two categories.

Not only is every aspect of the Christian faith now viewed primarily in relation to conservatism and liberalism, but these terms also have come increasingly to be employed in absolute fashion. There have long been well-defined scholarly positions called "conservative theology" and "liberal theology," but little attention is now being paid to these classic traditions. Instead, we regularly hear such affirmations as "I am a conservative" or "he is liberal," in which the assumption seems to be that these are religious terms with a specific content all their own. It is not too much to claim that, for many, the "conservative/liberal" conceptual framework has been elevated to the status of a dominant criterion for classifying faith that supersedes categories derived from more traditional sources such as Scripture or creed. In other words, there is a decided preference today to define one's ultimate value-orientation as conservative or liberal rather than as biblical or Baptist or Calvinist or other such designations.

We are now ready to summarize the theological situation that this book will seek to investigate. The prevailing assumptions among Southern Baptists in this generation, as well as among a number of other religious groups loosely called Evangelicals, are as follows:

• There are two basic perspectives or positions regarding the Christian faith that may be called conservative and liberal. The very nature and purpose of the Christian faith are compatible with one or the other of these categories, so that it is entirely appropriate to describe Christianity in terms of this conceptual framework.

• Not only are these appropriate categories in which to conceptualize the Christian faith, but they also are urgently important ones in which to do so. In other words, it matters greatly—for some it matters supremely—whether one's Christianity is conservative or liberal. Apparently, there is something inherent in these concepts that confers upon one's Christianity a validity that it otherwise would not have without it. The assumption is that one's faith is not just different, but is actually better or worse, by virtue of being either conservative or liberal in character.

• Finally, there is something mutually exclusive, even incompatible, between these two options. One cannot be both conservative and liberal at the same time. Instead, a great gulf is fixed that requires a fateful choice between absolute alternatives. So contradictory are these options that one of them is usually championed at the expense of the other. Thus, to be conservative carries with it the corollary notion that to be liberal is regrettable if not reprehensible. Indeed, some people read the drama of Christian history as a fight to the finish between conservatives and liberals as if they were, by nature, implacable foes.

I do not wish to exaggerate the situation simply for the sake of making this book seem more important. Instead, I would submit that the axioms just described are not only widely held but also, taken together, constitute a religious orientation with a theological agenda all its own. Measured against the sweep of Christian history, the notion of believers as conservative or liberal in the absolute sense that these terms are being used today is a twentieth-century innovation. What we are dealing with here is nothing less than a new kind of Christian self-understanding unique to the contemporary era.

For 1,900 years the disciples of Jesus Christ never understood or identified themselves either as conservatives or as liberals, yet, almost overnight, these code words have become the most crucial way to signal one's religious stance. A basic contention of this book is that this dramatic shift from classic religious categories to contemporary secular categories represents the most significant theological development among Southern Baptists in our generation.

Perhaps here is the most suitable point at which to clarify my own involvement in the situation under investigation. I do not write this book to advocate either conservatism or liberalism. My desire is to treat both positions with equal objectivity and fairness. I have many cherished friends who identify themselves either as conservatives or as liberals, and I fully respect these self-designations. My primary purpose, rather, is to subject both of these viewpoints to careful scrutiny in order to determine their adequacy as categories by which to describe the Christian faith. Nothing I say is designed to be polemical or even partisan in the arena called denominational politics. If anything, I hope to move in the opposite direction of adversaries on both sides of that fray. My method will not be to use either conservatism or liberalism as the criterion by which to judge my own faith or that of others. Rather, I shall attempt to turn the tables, as it were, in using the normative substance of our common faith as the criterion by which to judge both conservatism and liberalism.

II

If I am at all correct in my contention that the rise of a religion of conservatism opposed to one of liberalism is the most significant theological development in the recent history of Southern Baptist life, then it becomes astonishing how little serious attention has been given to this phenomenon. A check of the first eighteen volumes of the *Southern Baptist Periodical Index,* especially the meeting described above, shows that almost nothing had appeared on this subject between 1965-1982 in the forty-seven periodicals published by SBC agencies.[2]

A look through the catalogues of our leading seminary libraries reveals a complete absence of standard works on the nature and history of conservatism and liberalism in American life. For example, preparation of the Deere lectures on the subject of this book took me to the library of The Southern Baptist Theological Seminary in the early 1980s when a fierce battle was already raging over claims to "conservatism" in the seminary's sponsoring denomination. Accordingly, I spent my first day there orienting myself to the meaning of this divisive concept. The latest edition of *The Encyclopaedia Britannica* provided a core bibliography on the subject. Not a one of the works listed was in the seminary library.

Of necessity we must begin with the basic terms of the debate and inquire as to their meaning in the light of their history. Broadly speaking, conservatism and liberalism were first compared as conscious concepts to interpret the French Revolution of 1789, hence their original connotation was political. The actual terminology entered into English somewhat hesitantly around 1815-1825 and became fairly standard-ized after 1830, especially in Britain as a replacement for "Tory" and "Whig." Once established as political labels, the terms gradually accumu-lated philosophical, economic, and cultural connotations as well, with theological and religious applications beginning after 1850 but becom-ing widespread only in the twentieth century. Now for a bit more detail.

The acknowledged father of conservatism, though he never employed the term, was the Englishman Edmund Burke who, in his *Reflections on the Revolution in France* (1790),[3] "did more than any other thinker to turn the intellectual tide from a rationalist contempt for the past to a tradition-ist reverence for it."[4] A more extreme form of European conservatism was founded by the Frenchman Joseph M. de Maistre who, until his death in 1821, defended the *ancien regime* of "throne and altar" (monarchy and papacy). In America, counterparts to Burke were found among Federal-ists such as John Adams and Alexander Hamilton. After the demise of the Federalist Party in the early 1800s, a more reactionary form of conserva-tism similar to that of de Maistre surfaced among landowners, such as John C. Calhoun, in the South, where it lurks to this day.

The origins of liberalism are both more remote and more complex than those of conservatism and are to be sought in the long, slow struggle for individual rights that characterized seventeenth- and eighteenth-century European life, especially in England between the Glorious Revolution of 1688 and the Reform Act of 1867. We may begin with the quest for liberty of conscience that early involved Thomas Hobbes (*Leviathan*, 1651) and John Locke (*Letters Concerning Toleration*, 1689; *Second Treatise of Civil Government*, 1690) in Britain; Benedict de Spinoza (*Tractatus Theologigo-Politicus*, 1670) and Charles-Lewis de Montesquieu (*The Spirit of Laws*, 1748) on the Continent. During the latter part of the eighteenth century, with revolution in the air, concern for political freedoms came to the forefront, resulting in influential advances by thinkers such as Jean-Jacques Rousseau (*The Social Contract*, 1762) in France and John Stuart Mill (*On Liberty*, 1859) in England. Many of these insights were mediated to America through such voices as those of Thomas Paine and Thomas Jefferson, and later from the southern populist, Andrew Jackson.

In this formative phase, both concepts were relatively easy to understand. Liberalism arose earlier as the protest of an emerging middle class against the ancient and medieval system that restricted freedom of opportunity to an aristocratic elite limited primarily to royalty, clergy, and landed gentry. Beginning in the seventeenth century, the rich humanism fostered by the Renaissance and the Reformation began to be actively sought by aspiring merchants and professionals. A three-pronged attack against all forms of arbitrary authority demanded the following freedoms:

• political freedom of conscience, of privacy (noninterference), and of participation (enfranchisement) from the government
• religious freedom of toleration and of uncoerced belief from the church
• economic freedom of a self-adjusting market mechanism for consumers (Adam Smith) from the wealthy

In all of this, the key instinct was to support those structures that protected and developed the full potential of the individual but to limit those powers that inhibited or thwarted the individual by demanding subservience to a group or conformity to a social station determined by birth. In short, early liberalism sought to define a "Bill of Rights" that would give every person, regardless of class, the maximum freedom possible without jeopardizing the minimum requirements of the social contract.

In this struggle against centuries of oppression, it was inevitable that the Establishment would yield its privileges grudgingly. This recalcitrance produced conflict that occasionally erupted into violent revolution. The social anarchy accompanying the French Revolution of 1789 so convulsed the institutions of society that it precipitated the rise of conservatism as a protest of the feudal-aristocratic-agrarian classes against disruptive change. Advocates of this position argued the virtues of order and stability as the context for evolutionary improvement rather than revolutionary upheaval. They pointed to the tested continuities of tradition, to the strength of consensus based on shared experience, and to the curbs on human unruliness imposed by loyalty to the crown and reverence for the altar. Recoiling in horror from the rootlessness of untried innovation, conservatism was a plea to subordinate the unbridled passions of the moment to the accumulated and sifted wisdom of the ages.

Several important observations may be drawn from this brief historical survey of the earliest period of conservatism and liberalism. The first is that, viewed in their original context, certain features of both movements surely commend themselves to us. If conservatism originally meant a concern for stable, orderly society rooted in the most enduring traditions humanity had been able to develop, then who among us is not a conservative? But if liberalism originally meant a concern for human rights that would free the individual to develop his or her maximum potential, then who among us is not also a liberal? Which leads to a second observation: These two movements did not arise in opposition to each other; rather, each arose in opposition to the excesses of the other. Liberalism was not a protest against conservatism but against a reactionary medieval authoritarianism, dogmatism, and obscurantism that all of us would oppose. Likewise, conservatism was not a protest against true liberalism but against a reckless radicalism that all of us would abhor.

These two observations help to explain a third point; namely, that the same persons were often sympathetic with, and therefore active in, both movements. Those great harbingers of liberalism, Hobbes and Locke, were staunchly conservative in their attitude toward the crown. Conversely, even though the conservative Edmund Burke was no friend of popular democracy, denouncing it bitterly long before the Jacobin Terror reigned in France, he was nevertheless a Lockean liberal in politics and a *laissez-faire* liberal in economics whose ideas of free trade were at one with those of Adam Smith. In Germany, Johann Wolfgang von Goethe, as early as 1830, urged a mature synthesis between a conservative framework and liberal goals.

Indeed, even before the two movements achieved definitive form early in the nineteenth century, their constitutive elements had already been harmonized with each other in those remarkable documents called the Declaration of Independence and the Constitution of the United States. The former, drawn up primarily by Thomas Jefferson, was a model of the democratic-utopian rhetoric of liberalism, while the latter, under the influence of the Federalists, counter-balanced that emphasis with Burkean conservatism. If the American experience means anything, it means that conservatism and liberalism are not mutually exclusive![5]

The War of Independence was a classic example of revolutionary conservatism that, unlike the French Revolution of 1789, won the approbation of thoughtful liberals and conservatives alike. In one sense, the unique genius of our Founding Fathers was to transcend the tired cleavages of Europe by fusing into one national lifestyle the best features of both movements, thereby creating a society in dynamic equilibrium characterized by historical continuity, organic development, and orderly progress. Historically speaking, to be an American means to be both conservative and liberal at the same time in the finest sense of both terms.

History, however, does not stand still, and since conservatism and liberalism arose as reactions to extremes—of anarchy on the one hand and of authoritarianism on the other—both continued to react to new circumstances that were often dramatically different from those that originally called them into being. This led, in many cases, to a curious role reversal by which the liberalism of one generation becomes the conservatism of the next, and vice versa.

Take, for example, the central issue of the role of government in the lives of its citizens. Conservatism clearly began in support of strong government, viewed as a hereditary monarchy with vested rights of absolute veto over any plebiscite; while liberalism just as clearly began in support of limited government, insisting that the state not do for individuals what they could do for themselves. But over the past two hundred years, participatory democracy so completely triumphed on American soil that conservatives were forced to abandon their high doctrine of the state, rooted in the divine right of kings and the established church, and became instead the champions of limited government except in the area of national defense. Conversely, no sooner had conservatives ceased to champion the state than liberals latched onto it as the only mechanism powerful enough to guarantee enfranchisement for the masses, and so they have become—since Franklin D. Roosevelt—the advocates of big government!

For the careful student of history, there is a certain internal consistency to these role reversals. But to the general public, such sweeping changes serve only to provoke wholesale confusion. In the fall of 1976, responding to the growing importance of these terms for issues raised by a presidential election, the journal *Commentary* asked a wide-ranging group of American intellectuals with varying viewpoints to contribute to a symposium on "What Is a Liberal—Who Is a Conservative?"[6]

One overwhelming conclusion emerged from the sixty-four responses: There was no consensus on what these terms meant as used at that time. Both concepts were undergoing a sea change of meaning, and the result was semantic bedlam. For example, Alfred Kazin called them "commonly fraudulent and intellectually useless terms."[7] Jeane Kirkpatrick described them as "devoid of specific meaning, laden with affect, entangled in fashion, and involved in an ongoing power struggle of momentous importance."[8] Lewis Lapham concluded that "because the words no longer possess legitimate meaning, it has become impossible to introduce oneself as either a liberal or a conservative. . . . in their unqualified state, the words can be assigned only to one's enemies."[9]

Two insights of great importance for our purposes may be drawn from this climate of confusion. The first is that Southern Baptists began to transform these tortured terms into key theological watchwords at precisely that period in history when their meanings had become hopelessly obscure to thinking persons. Hear Lapham again:

> Like most words that express prejudice rather than thought, they offer more information about the person who employs them than they do about the people on whom they fall like stones. In common usage this has resulted in the presence of two negative caricatures. Although it has become all but impossible to meet a liberal or a conservative, it has become difficult to avoid the anti-liberal and the anti-conservative.[10]

A second observation is based on the reactionary, even polemical, way in which these slippery terms continue being used today. Any meaningful discussion of their merits must be based on the essential and hence enduring significance of these concepts rather than on some contextual and hence transient significance that may disappear tomorrow. So volatile have these labels become, and so expediently are they being employed to prove a point in some power struggles, that one must almost "date" the particular conservatism or liberalism being defended or attacked in order for it to have any meaning.

But can we rescue the concepts of conservatism and liberalism from the relativities of time and define their inner essence in such a way that the normative meaning of each may then be subjected to a Christian critique? Difficult as the task appears, I believe that it can be done. For, at bottom, these emphases reflect an enduring issue of human experience that goes back at least to the time of Parmenides and Heraclitus (early fifth century B.C.).

Parmenides of Elea argued that reality is unalterable, and therefore indivisible, continuous, and motionless. Which meant that change is logically inconceivable, and therefore illusory, contradictory, and unreal. Heraclitus of Ephesus, on the other hand, held that reality is in constant flux, like a flowing river, and therefore a process of incessant motion and unending development. Which meant that change is of the essence of reality, a continuous interaction and reciprocity of opposites necessary to the balance of nature. By stressing the changeless, Parmenides became the archetypal apostle of conservatism, while Heraclitus, by stressing change, became the harbinger of an eventual liberalism.

It is in their respective attitudes toward change that we find the most distinctive features of each position and the most crucial differences between them. The word "conservatism" comes from a root referring to weapons or armor and so connotes that which protects from change or destruction. As Webster's "Unabridged" puts it, conservatism is that point of view that "advocates preservation of the established order and views proposals for change critically and usually with distrust."[11] The word "liberalism," on the other hand, comes from a root meaning to grow, and so implies a process of development that reflects, to quote Webster again, a commitment to progress "not bound by authoritarianism, orthodoxy, or traditional or established forms."[12]

At the level of instinct, conservatives resist change on the conviction that what is known and approved is more likely, on balance, to be acceptable than what is unknown and untested. Liberals, by contrast, welcome change because their contentment with the status quo is not as strong as their conviction that change, even though untried, will bring improvements never before realized.

From these fundamentally different orientations toward the past and the future come a number of related characteristics that tend to typify the two positions. Taken as a cluster, each constitutes what might be called an "ideology" embodied in a "lifestyle" representative of the respective positions. I have prepared a chart placed at the end of this chapter utilizing descriptive terminology for each position. A comparison of each will show that conservatism and liberalism differ in emphasis between experience and intuition, realism and idealism, unity and diversity, particularism and universalism, conformity and nonconformity.

If this swift sketch is at all correct, then we may say, despite the confusion of our time, that conservatism and liberalism are coherent concepts with definable content; that they embody a wide range of significant options in human consciousness; and that they are therefore worthy of the most careful analysis, not only in terms of political, economic, and philosophical theory, but also in terms of a Christian critique. How may this be done?

III

There are three normative sources from which to draw when attempting to bring the Christian faith to bear on any reality under investigation. First and foremost is the biblical revelation as recorded in Holy Scripture. Second is the rich heritage of Christian history, the lived experience of the People of God with the Word of God across the ages. Third is the doctrine expressed by the church in its confessional formulations and theological reflections. Standard practice when developing a critique is, first, to discover all of the biblical, historical, and theological teachings on the subject at hand; then to synthesize these insights into a coherent Christian position; and, finally, to compare the results with the way in which the subject is viewed in contemporary thought. Such an approach usually leads both to a fresh clarification of Christian teaching on a given subject and to an evaluation of the adequacy with which that subject is understood in human thought.

A major problem arises when we try to treat conservatism and liberalism in this fashion, however, because these concepts do not appear in any of our normative Christian sources. Neither of the terms appear in either the Old Testament or the New Testament as rendered in any standard English translation. As post-Enlightenment concepts, they are obviously not at issue in any of the great crises of church history. We never find them mentioned by Irenaeus, Origen, Augustine, Aquinas, Luther, or Calvin. Nor do they find expression in any of the great creeds of the church. Likewise, they are conspicuously lacking in all of our denominational confessions of faith. A search of the major systematic theologies yields the same meager results.

Here we are confronted with a methodological impasse of the first magnitude created by the fact that many Baptists are now making central to their expression of the faith a pair of concepts that have never played a part in the formulation of Christian truth. Talk about irony! We are a "People of the Book," yet the favorite way in which many are now declaring this fidelity is in terms not drawn from that Book. We glory in the "historic Baptist position," yet many are doing so in categories ignored by that tradition itself.

In recent years we have exalted the 1963 or 2000 Baptist Faith and Message statement almost to the status of a creed, yet many have done so in the name of a position on which these doctrinal summaries are completely silent. It is schizophrenic to champion biblical supremacy, historical confessionalism, and theological orthodoxy in terms of a conservatism or a liberalism that is neither defined nor controlled by any of these three normative sources!

If our criteria for testing Christian faith have nothing explicit to say about either conservatism or liberalism, then how may we use these three sources to measure the adequacy of what today is being called a "conservative faith" or a "liberal faith"? Obviously, we shall have to go behind these modern terms and inquire into what sacred Scripture, church history, and orthodox theology have to say about such themes identified by our chart. In short, we shall have to probe Christian attitudes toward past and future in the unfolding process of time. Is our faith fundamentally a home or a horizon? An anchor or an adventure? A deposit "once for all delivered to the saints" (Jude 3) or a declaration that "it does not yet appear what we shall be" (1 John 3:1)?

The next three chapters will seek to address these issues by doing something that is at once both conservative and liberal. In true conservative fashion, we shall focus on those givens of our faith that have been central to a Christian self-understanding for centuries. But at the same time, in true liberal fashion, we shall put new questions to these venerable sources, questions posed by the distinctively modern phenomenon of conservatism and liberalism. Thus will the very method of our inquiry join these two polarities in a creative symbiosis, perhaps thereby modeling the way in which they should coexist within the household of faith.

Conservatism	Liberalism
Being	Becoming
Compromise	Criticism
Continuity	Change
Dependability	Development
Elitism	Egalitarianism
Fidelity	Flux
Heritage	Hope
Nostalgia	Novelty
Order	Originality
Power	Potentiality
Presentation	Progress
Security	Speculation
Stability	Spontaneity
Structure	Spirit
Tradition	Transformation

Notes

[1] Eyewitness report by the author, who participated in both meetings of October 5 and November 12, 1982. Each of the participants in this illustration has confirmed its accuracy to the author.

[2] Lynn E. May, Jr., et. al., eds., *Southern Baptist Periodical Index*, vols. 1-18 (Nashville: Historical Commission of the Southern Baptist Convention, 1965-1982).

[3] Edmund Burke, *Reflections on the Revolution in France*, with an introduction by Russell Kirk (Chicago: Gateway Editions, 1955).

[4] Peter Viereck, "Conservatism," *The New Encyclopaedia Britannica: Macropaedia*, 15th ed., 5 (Chicago: Encyclopaedia Britannica, 1982): 63.

[5] In a brilliant essay on definition, "Conservatism as an Ideology," *The American Political Science Review*, 51:454-473, 1957, Samuel P. Huntington shows why "Burke

equaled Locke" in America as well as in England (461) and comments, "No necessary dichotomy exists . . . between conservatism and liberalism. . . . The true enemy of the conservative is not the liberal but the extreme radical" (460).

[6]Norman Podhoretz, ed., "What Is a Liberal—Who Is a Conservative?" *Commentary*, 62 (September 1976): 31-113.

[7]Ibid., 71.

[8]Ibid., 72.

[9]Ibid., 75.

[10]Ibid.

[11]Philip B. Gove, ed., *Webster's Third New International Dictionary of the English Language* (Springfield, MA: G. & C. Merriam, 1976), 483.

[12]Ibid., 1303.

CHAPTER 2

A Biblical Critique of
Conservatism and Liberalism

Based on a general orientation to the meaning of the modern terms "conservatism" and "liberalism" provided by our introductory chapter, we are now ready to launch a distinctively Christian critique of these two concepts. It is inevitable that we begin this task with the Bible. Our concern, however, will not be to take either a conservative or a liberal approach to Scripture, as many claim to do, but rather to take a scriptural approach to conservatism and liberalism. Rather than prejudicing or even predetermining the outcome of our investigation by superimposing either one of these contemporary ideological categories on Scripture as a presupposition, let us instead allow the Bible to evaluate the adequacy of these two competing viewpoints as their contribution to a Christian perspective.

I propose to look first at the Bible as a whole, then at each of its two Testaments separately, asking whether the central characteristic of Scripture has more affinity with the perspective that we now call conservatism or with the one called liberalism. Our purpose, in other words, will not be to determine whether we happen to be conservative or liberal at heart, but to determine whether the deepest instincts of biblical faith are conservative or liberal at heart. That, after all, is far more important than whatever personal position we may happen to take based on contemporary influences.

I

When we view the entire sweep of Scripture and inquire as to its essential shape, the most fundamental finding to be considered is that the Bible is divided into an Old Testament and a New Testament.[1] There are two basic parts, always clearly distinguished and never intermingled, yet together they constitute a basic unity. As far as we know, early Christians never considered the possibility of including their writings as part of the

Jewish canon, as if they could be one and the same, and yet, except for early efforts by heretics such as Marcion, they never considered the possibility of collecting their sacred writings apart from the Jewish canon, as if they could stand alone. We must now ponder what it means for our Bible to be both "Old" and "New" and yet one.

From the outset, the Old Testament was clearly sacred Scripture for apostolic Christianity. This may be visually grasped from the study of a Greek New Testament that sets Old Testament quotations and allusions in special type. Johann Perk, for example, counts 2,688 Old Testament parallels in the New Testament.[2] But beyond the sheer quantity of usage, the qualitative impact of the Old Testament on New Testament faith may be glimpsed from a formula that underlies the earliest Christian confessions, "according to the Scriptures" (1 Cor. 15:3-4). This suggests, in the words of C. H. Dodd, that the Old Testament furnished "the sub-structure of New Testament theology."[3]

While it might seem natural for the earliest Jewish Christians in Palestine to make such a profound use of their inherited Scriptures, we must remember that the Old Testament played a pivotal part in the Gentile mission as well. The Apostle Paul, for example, not only made extensive use of it in his synagogue preaching, but also constantly referred to it in his letters to predominantly Gentile churches. For example, in writing to the recently converted Graeco-Roman pagans of Corinth, Paul simply assumed their kinship with the Hebrew patriarchs who participated in the exodus from Egypt: "I want you to know, brethren, that *our fathers* were all under the cloud, and all passed through the sea, and all were baptized into Moses in the cloud and in the sea" (1 Cor. 10:1-2). It is remarkable how complete an identification with the Old Testament Paul here presupposes on the part of his readers.

After AD 70, the center of gravity of the Christian movement shifted decisively from Judaism to Hellenism. Predominantly Gentile converts found themselves with a seemingly provincial Bible full of the genealogies of Jewish tribes that no longer existed, of the exploits of a Jewish monarchy that no longer ruled, and of the rituals of a Jewish temple that no longer stood. Moreover, these Scriptures were still the sacred literature of a largely discredited and even despised Jewish religion that had sought to stamp out the emerging Christian faith through violent persecution and had, more recently, engaged in armed insurrection against the constituted authority of Rome. From this distance, we may not fully appreciate what an enormous liability it was for Gentile Christians in the late first century to retain the Old Testament as their only Bible.

And yet cling to it they did, not just for a century and more while they were collecting their own canon, but for all of the centuries since then, even after the completed New Testament became available and approved to serve as the authoritative guide to Christian faith and practice. This tenacious retention of Jewish scripture by Gentile Christians as an integral part of their canon must be viewed as a strongly conservative instinct, a refusal to jettison the spiritual heritage of their faith even after its form had become for them almost completely anachronistic. To this day, the existence of an "Old" Testament within the Christian Bible says that our faith is profoundly rooted in a past that must never be allowed to become alien history but must always tell the story of "*our* fathers" in the faith.

And yet, beside that "Old" Testament there stands another Testament that we call "New." Indeed, precisely because the Jewish Scriptures were "Old," their very retention implied the necessity of developing a Christian counterpart that would be truly "New." After all, that was the hallmark of the religion of Jesus: Everything about it was *new*—not only a new covenant (1 Cor. 11:25; Heb. 8:13, 9:15) but also a new creation (2 Cor. 5:17, Gal. 6:15) that involved a new birth (John 3:3), a new nature (Eph. 4:24), a new humanity (Eph. 2:15), and finally a new heaven and a new earth (Rev. 21:1). The second Testament was aptly called "New" because it held within itself the religion of him who taught that new wine cannot be put into old wineskins (Mark 2:22).

Ironically, after two thousand years, Christianity and its Scriptures have been "new" for so long that even the newness has come to be taken for granted. What was once a revolutionary rhetoric of transformation is now repeated as a routine statement of the status quo. After two millennia we talk about the "New" Testament with no sense of its *newness* but only with a sense of its *oldness*, as if the "new" had somehow worn off centuries ago. What we urgently need today is a fresh awareness that, just as the Old Testament is really *old*, the New Testament is still really *new!* In an effort to recover the sense of newness that pervaded early Christianity, I propose to take what may well be the three most central bulwarks of Old Testament religion and show how they were transformed in the New Testament church.

(1) From earliest antiquity, *circumcision* was practiced among the Hebrews as a religious ceremony acknowledging their covenant with

God (Gen. 17:1-27). As the centuries passed, it assumed ever greater importance as a mark of fidelity in resisting the threat of assimilation with the heathen. By the time of the first century, it was the preeminent act of initiation into the commonwealth of Israel for Jews and proselytes alike. As Paul put it, to the Jewish mind there were only two kinds of people in this world: the "circumcised" and the "uncircumcised" (Eph. 2:11). This rite determined one's basic identity in the sight of God.

In light of the importance attached to circumcision in Judaism, it is astonishing that Christianity dropped the practice almost as soon as it moved out into the Hellenistic world. Paul, who had been duly circumcised as a Jew in infancy (Phil. 3:5), argued strongly for its elimination (Rom. 2:28; 1 Cor. 7:19; Gal. 5:6, 6:15). After the time of Paul, the church simply began to ignore a rite that had enjoyed the sanction of Scripture for centuries. We shall return to circumcision in chapter 5 because of its relevance to other themes in this book.

(2) Almost as old as the Jewish devotion to circumcision was its veneration of a *centralized shrine*, first the Tabernacle of Moses, then the Temple of Solomon. It would be hard to think of any institution that more completely dominated the religious life of the Old Testament. Long sections of the Pentateuch were devoted to its priesthood and ritual. The historical books described its building and subsequent fortunes. Many of the prophets were devoted to its preservation (Isaiah) or purification (Jeremiah), while others looked forward to its restoration (Haggai, Zechariah). The Psalter was the worship book of the cultus, with the late apocalypses prefiguring its eventual perfection. With all of this biblical attention lavished on the Temple, it is not surprising that, by the first century, it was the unifying center of worldwide Judaism, the political and economic pivot of national life, and the supreme symbol of Judaism's claim to the presence of God within its midst.

Despite this exalted status, however, the entire cultic apparatus— Temple, priesthood, and sacrifice—disappeared from Christianity almost as soon as the daughter faith spread beyond the environs of Jerusalem. Long before its physical facilities were destroyed in AD 70, the Temple was superseded in Christian worship as a result of the claim of Paul that all of his struggling Gentile congregations constituted a true sanctuary of God's presence (Eph. 2:21-22), and that his immature converts were all a holy priesthood who could offer their very lives as a sacrifice acceptable unto God (Rom. 12:1).

(3) Finally, it is a similar story in regard to the Jewish *Sabbath*. Firmly rooted in the Mosaic Decalogue (Exod. 20:8), this holy day came to take on enormous importance during the Exile when, lacking any Temple at which to worship, the Jews were forced to assert their religious distinctiveness primarily through weekly Sabbath observance. Even after the Exile most Jews were unable to enjoy regular access to the Jerusalem Temple, hence obedience to a growing number of Sabbath regulations became the most practical way to demonstrate one's fidelity to the Torah. It is not surprising, therefore, that the indifference of Jesus to Sabbath scruple led to deadly controversy with the religious leaders of his day (Mark 2:23–3:6).

Despite these clashes, Jesus never repudiated the Sabbath as such, yet his followers soon shifted away from its observance in favor of Sunday as the day on which their Lord had risen. The peculiar thing to notice about this change is that it was never given explicit justification anywhere in the New Testament. Early Christians felt free to set aside a central feature of the Old Testament without bothering to explain how they could do so in the absence of any specific command or even suggestion from their Lord to that effect. Yet, in so doing, they continued to attribute to the Old Testament the highest possible authority as Scripture.

Let us pause at this point to ponder the implications of these three illustrations. Seen against a first-century background when circumcision, Temple, and Sabbath were of paramount importance to the parent faith, it is amazing that all three of these venerable institutions were set aside in less than one generation by its offspring. To be sure, the deeper meanings they conveyed were retained in spiritualized form, but the practices themselves disappeared from the Christian religion, and it was precisely their practice that was mandated throughout the Old Testament. For comparable changes to take place in Christian life today, it would be necessary for us to replace baptism as our rite of initiation, decentralization as our pattern of organization, and Sunday as our day of worship—and to make all of these changes within the present generation without benefit of scriptural injunction!

If one argues that radical departures of this magnitude were utterly impractical within so short a time frame, along with being unwarranted by Scripture, we can only reply that the early church made changes just that drastic in their abandonment of circumcision as the rite of initiation, of one centralized Temple as the pattern of organization, and of

Saturday as the day of worship. Furthermore, they made all of these changes within one generation of transition from Jewish to Hellenistic Christianity (c. AD 40-80), and they did so despite hundreds of passages in their Bible supporting the practices that were being terminated. All of which is to say, with more forcefulness than is often employed, that the New Testament is really *new*; that it represents nothing less than an eschatological fulfillment of the faith of Israel and, therefore, that it reflects not only continuities but also dramatic discontinuities with all that had gone before.

In terms of our primary agenda, this astonishing sense of newness that suddenly appeared in but a moment of history must be reckoned as one of the greatest liberal achievements of all time. For one brief epoch it was as if futurity had invaded the present, enabling a courageous band to transcend the restraints of tradition and accelerate the pace of change. What we have just described was not a process of cautious evolution but of radical mutation, a quantum leap from the Old Age of promise to the New Age of fulfillment. Therefore, just as the permanent presence of an "Old" Testament in the Christian canon means that we are to be forever conservative in retaining our ancient heritage, the permanent presence of a "New" Testament in that same canon means that we are to be forever liberal in living in advance of the age to come.

Which brings us back to the central point made at the outset of this discussion; namely, that our Bible is both "Old" and "New" and yet is also *one*. The unity of the canon means that the conservatism implied in having an Old Testament and the liberalism implied in having a New Testament are thereby set in dynamic equilibrium, for one axiom of a Christian hermeneutic is that each Testament must always be read in the light of the other. To accept the Bible as a whole is to accept the task of being both conservative and liberal at the same time!

II

With this broad overview of the entire Bible behind us, let us look now within each Testament in an effort to grasp whether its central dynamic is conservative or liberal. As in the discussion just concluded, it is important not to search for obscure proof texts to prove a point, or to emphasize some marginal development of brief duration, but rather to identify the dominant perspective of each Testament and then ask what light it sheds on our agenda.

Viewed most comprehensively, the Old Testament resembles an ellipse with two foci: Exodus and Exile. No other experiences more profoundly affected the course of Hebrew history. Taken together, they created a dialectic whose meaning was constitutive of Israelite religion. Exodus stood for God's redemption, for those mighty acts by which he had delivered his people from oppression and entered into covenant with them to be a holy nation. Exile, on the other hand, stood for divine judgment of the people for their failure to keep the covenant, and hence for their hope of restoration and renewal. Now let us look more closely at the internal dynamics of this dialectic of mercy and punishment.

The Exodus from Egypt became for Israel a paradigmatic event that enshrined its most sacred memories of God's gracious dealings with his people. As such, it served as the founding epoch in a theology of salvation history and hence as the core of Israel's earliest confessions of faith (Deut. 26:5-9). At least annually, its central drama was reenacted in the festivals of Passover and Tabernacles. As the actual circumstances of the Exodus receded into the distant past, its meaning became idealized in religious practice. This caused Israel increasingly to cherish, at least in theory, a return to those conditions that had existed in the Mosaic era.

What this means is that the Exodus came increasingly to play a conservative role in Old Testament religion. It kept alive the wilderness wanderings when Israel was a semi-nomadic people dwelling in tents (Num. 33:1-49). This reinforced the prophetic disdain for sedentary Canaanite society that came to its most radical expression in the Rechabites (Jer. 35:1-19). It also encouraged a veneration of the tribal confederation with its democratic decentralization, prompting the aged Samuel to oppose the plea of the people for an earthly monarch presiding over a centralized kingdom (2 Sam. 8:1-22, 12:1-25). The strength of this nostalgic strain may perhaps be seen best in the fact that when Israel was carried into captivity some 700 years after the original Exodus, it instinctively viewed its longed-for liberation primarily in terms of a New Exodus (Isa. 40-55).

Which brings us to the crisis of the Exile as the incubator of a decisively new attitude toward the future within Israelite religion. This emergence of true futurity took place in several stages over many years, but its chief catalyst was the destruction of monarchy and cultus by the Babylonians in the sixth century B.C. In the pre-exile period, the prophets of doom had come with increasing certainty to the conviction that the nation would be destroyed at the hands of its enemies, which meant a decisive rupture with all of the continuities of the past. Because of their unshakable faith in the sovereignty and purposes of God, Isaiah and his followers (e.g., Jeremiah) held out the hope that a remnant would be spared to forge a new covenant.

After catastrophe fell, this thread of promise was enlarged into a hope that, with God's help, a repentant people would return to reestablish the kingdom of their father David in all its splendor. The more that this religio-political hope was nourished, the more it came to be couched in cosmic terms, as if this restoration in Palestine would establish the kingly reign of God over all the earth. It was but a short step from such poetic descriptions of Israel's future glory to a full-blown eschatology that saw the whole of historical tragedy transformed by its replacement with a new heaven and a new earth.

Because the Exile brutally destroyed those structures that had perpetuated Israel's past, it thereby invested Israel's future with a significance it had never known before. Rather than renounce an ancient covenant whose promises were now in shambles, the faithful remnant decided instead to postpone into the indefinite future those blessings that had obviously been denied them in the present. This shift represented neither the wishful thinking of national hubris nor the esoteric speculation based on Zoroastrian dualism, but a stubborn refusal to give up on God even when he seemed excluded from the historical process. In this trial the remnant learned that Yahweh was a God of disaster, and hence of discontinuity; just as he was a God of blessings, and of continuity. It learned that faith meant not only living in the present out of what God had already done in the past, but also living in the present out of what he would yet do in the future.

As a result of the Exile, therefore, Israel's religious vision now became bipolar, both looking back to an essential and meaningful past and looking forward to an equally essential and meaningful future. In terms of our agenda, this means that the Exile was basically a liberal epoch in Israel's experience for at least two reasons. On the one hand, it showed Israel that even its most sacred traditions of the past could be utterly swept away; and, on the other hand, it gave Israel an unshakable confidence that, no matter how glorious the past had been, the best was yet to be. Despite the repeated calamities that followed restoration, Israel never gave up on this hope but rather enriched and intensified it as one of the most significant legacies of the Old Testament to the New.

This conclusion does not mean that Old Testament eschatological thought was inherently "liberal" in the sense of being progressive, innovative, even radical. (Witness, for example, the "restorationist" eschatology of Ezekiel 40-48 that breathed the conservative spirit of Ezra and Nehemiah.) Rather, it means that eschatological thought did open up to Israel entirely new possibilities for expressing the importance of the future, thereby creating a tension with the traditional veneration of the past that gives the Old Testament its distinctive character.

III

We have just seen that the Old Testament is built in bipolar fashion around Exodus and Exile, thereby setting conservatism and liberalism in dynamic equilibrium as influences on its religious thought. The New Testament might well be similarly described as an ellipse with two foci: namely, the tension between Jewish and Hellenistic Christianity. Viewed historically, the most fundamental question with which the New Testament deals is what it means for a movement that was born entirely within Judaism to move completely beyond Judaism in less than one century.

The roots of this issue go back to the crisis of the Exile we were just considering. Once the collapse of history taught the post-exilic remnant to look beyond history for its eventual redemption, a few brave spirits began to realize that earthly affairs need never be the same again. Transcending the restorationist program of Ezra and Nehemiah, who wanted to put things back as they had always been, writers of books such as Jonah and Ruth began to call the people of God to a more spacious conception of their mission not limited to the land of Palestine or confined within the walls of Jerusalem. Thus began that fateful bifurcation between particularism and universalism that divided the Pharisees and Jesus. It was this duality, deep within its Jewish heritage, over which the early church was forced to struggle in determining its destiny as the New Israel of God (Gal. 6:16).

Clearly, Christianity began as a sectarian or reform movement entirely within Judaism. Not only was its founder a Jew, but so were all of his original apostles (Acts 1:21-26). From the outset it ministered within the framework of Jewish law, which included circumcision, Temple worship, and Sabbath observance (Acts 2:46-47). Fresh impetus was given to this Jewish element in AD 44 when James succeeded Peter as leader of the

Jerusalem church, in part because of his blood kinship with Jesus (Acts 12:17). Maurice Goguel went so far as to suppose that, with this rather sudden shift, apostolic Christianity was supplanted by dynastic Christianity of a type that would later reappear in the Islamic Caliphate.[4] With James in control, an extremist group of Pharisaic believers, usually called Judaizers, apparently felt free to challenge anyone—even Peter and Paul!—who seemed to compromise a strict Jewish understanding of the faith (Gal. 2:12, Acts 15:1-5). Supporting their strong separatist stance was a congregation that Acts described as "many thousands among the Jews who have believed [and] are all zealous for the law" (21:20).

In understanding this situation, we must remember that the period between the death of Herod Agrippa in AD 44 and the fall of Jerusalem in AD 70 was one of extreme political unrest throughout Palestine. Jerusalem was a hotbed of nationalistic hopes fanned by revolutionary fervor. A spirit of uprising was in the air that pitted Jew against Gentile without regard to religious affiliation. To use more contemporary terminology, this was a reactionary era when far-right political passion swept everything before it, demanding the most conservative religious zealotism to give divine sanction to what was fast becoming a holy war. In such an atmosphere, it is not surprising that Jewish Christianity centered in Jerusalem was very conservative in almost every commonly accepted connotation of that term.

At this point, the interesting thing to notice was that a counterthrust of liberalism came, not from some entirely different geographical area or religious background, but from within the very bosom of Jerusalem Christianity. As early as Acts 6 we learn that there was an identifiable group of Hellenists within that fellowship, one of whose leaders was Stephen, doubtless a Jew of the Diaspora as indicated by his association with the synagogue of the Freedmen (6:9). Defending himself against the charge of undermining both Temple and Torah (6:13), this heretofore unknown member of the Seven delivered the longest sermon recorded in the book of Acts (7:1-53) that even the cautious scholar, F. F. Bruce, called the most radical manifesto in the New Testament.[5] Ironically, Stephen's arguments "served only to confirm the charges brought against him."[6] Based on a daring reading of the Old Testament itself, he insisted that one fixed Temple in Jerusalem had been a mistake from the beginning, since it represented a departure from the portable Tabernacle of the Exodus wanderings (7:44-48). The stoning that sealed Stephen's fate as the first Christian martyr testified to an understanding by his enemies as calling for the immediate abolition of those ancestral customs sanctified by Scripture for centuries.

The blasphemous "heresy" of Stephen led not only to his untimely death but also to "a great persecution" that had the unwitting effect of scattering his Christian radicalism throughout the larger region (Acts 8:1). Soon the embryonic faith found its way to the pivotal city of Antioch, and in that cosmopolitan setting the gospel was extended directly to Greeks (Acts 11:19-21). Their ready response of faith meant that, for the first time, the church began to accept "a great number" (11:21) who had never had any prior contact with Judaism and who were not required to accept any purely Jewish practices as the condition of their discipleship. This innovation forced the issue that soon came to lie at the heart of the Pauline mission, namely: Out of the vast heritage of Old Testament religion, what was essential and what was optimal for the Christian believer? It will be immediately obvious that this is precisely the conservative/liberal question in its clearest expression.

The Jerusalem Conference of Acts 15 is often viewed as a summit meeting called to resolve this issue, at which time a compromise was worked out acceptable to all concerned. The meeting might better be described as an occasion at which selected leaders reported on how God had already settled the matter in terms of the realities of evangelistic practice. Peter, Barnabas, and Paul related that God had, in fact, repeatedly given his Holy Spirit and cleansed the hearts of Gentiles entirely by faith without regard to Jewish religious regulations, thus declaring them *de facto* unnecessary even if found in Scripture. James, for his part, agreed that Gentiles who turn to God need not be troubled with such requirements as circumcision, but he did urge them to avoid any offensive behavior that would scandalize their Jewish brethren. Adolph Schlatter well described the consistent position taken by all of the chief protagonists at this gathering: "St. Paul did in his sphere of activity exactly what St. James did in his. As James took care that the Jewish Christian should remain a Jew, and not turn into a Greek, so Paul insisted that the Greek Christian should remain a Greek and not pretend to be a Jew."[7]

When we step back to set the Jerusalem Conference within the framework of the entire book of Acts, we discover that its author has given us one of the most carefully nuanced treatises on conservatism and liberalism to be found in the New Testament. In one sense, Acts serves as a bridge between the almost entirely Jewish origins of Christianity in the ministry of Jesus and the almost entirely Gentile expression of the faith in the missionary churches of Paul. And what does this unique link between Gospels and Epistles tell us about the proper attitude toward this most momentous of all changes from Jewish to Gentile Christianity? Two things above all others: first, that a wide spectrum of opinion is both legitimate and desirable because, second, such diversity allows for creativity in responding to the missionary imperative of the gospel.

Let us consider that spectrum for a moment. James had to insist on conservatism in Jerusalem, or Christianity would have perished prematurely in that Jewish tinderbox. Paul had to take the liberalism of Stephen to Corinth, or the gospel would not have taken root in that pagan soil. But ultimately, Luke honored every position on this spectrum because God had already authenticated their divergent approaches by giving true converts to conservatives and liberals alike! That did not mean that all positions were legitimate, however, even if they led to Christian converts. Acts and the letters of Paul are deafening in their silence of any approval given to the extreme conservatism of the Judaizers in Palestine or to the extreme liberalism of the Gnosticizers in the Graeco-Roman world. Ironically, both of these movements were popular, as simplistic positions often are, perhaps a majority in its churches of Jerusalem and Corinth. But both James and Paul failed to be swayed by the temper of their times. At most, they could be described as a tampered or chastened conservative and liberal.

In this chapter we have sought the largest possible picture of biblical reality, and in every case we have found it to be bipolar: in Scripture as a whole, an "Old" Testament and a "New"; in the former of these, an Exodus and an Exile; in the latter of these, a Jewish Christianity and a Gentile Christianity. But the most remarkable thing we have found is that, in every case, this polarity corresponded to the tensions inherent in the differences between conservatism and liberalism. Which means, contrary to the unexamined theological assumptions of our day, that the two are not mutually contradictory. Rather, each requires the other to maintain its balance, and therefore each honors the other as full partners in honoring Christ, who is "the same yesterday and today and forever" (Heb. 13:8).

Notes

[1] The Jewish scriptures are called *palaia diathēkē* in 2 Corinthians 3:14, but, of course, the Christian scriptures are not yet called *kainē diathēkē* within the New Testament itself. The ambiguous meaning of *diathēkē* as either "covenant" or "testament" caused it to be rendered *testamentum* in Latin, hence "testament" in English, although "covenant" is a preferable translation.

[2] Johann Perk, *Handbuch zum Neuen Testament: Alttestamentliche Parallelen* (Angermund: "Der Pfug" Julius Nüttgens, 1947).

[3] C. H. Dodd, *According to the Scriptures: The Sub-structure of New Testament Theology* (London: Nisbet, 1952).

[4] Maurice Goguel, *The Birth of Christianity* (London: George Allen & Unwin, 1953), 113.

[5] F. F. Bruce, *Peter, Stephen, James, and John: Studies in Early Non-Pauline Christianity* (Grand Rapids: William B. Eerdmans, 1980), 52-57.

[6] Ibid., 55.

[7] Adolf Schlatter, *The Church in the New Testament Period* (London: S.P.C.K., 1955), 59.

CHAPTER 3

A Historical Critique
of Conservatism and Liberalism

For forty-eight years, Will and Ariel Durant toiled on their eleven-volume *Story of Civilization* that, in 2,000,000 words on 10,000 pages, sought to mediate the rich legacy of the past to a largely rootless twentieth-century world.[1] In a slender epilogue summing up their epic enterprise, titled *The Lessons of History*, the Durants concluded:

> Out of every hundred new ideas ninety-nine or more will probably be inferior to the traditional responses which they propose to replace. No one man, however brilliant or well informed, can come in one lifetime to such fullness of understanding as to safely judge and dismiss the customs or institutions of his society, for these are the wisdom of generations after centuries of experiment in the laboratory of history.
> . . . the conservative who resists change is as valuable as the radical who proposes it—perhaps as much more valuable as roots are more vital than grafts. It is good that new ideas should be heard, for the sake of the few that can be used; but it is also good that new ideas should be compelled to go through the mill of objection, opposition, and contumely; this is the trial heat which innovations must survive before being allowed to enter the human race.[2]

I have chosen to begin with these quotations because they so felicitously express what many historians take to be the innate conservatism of history. After all, do not the accumulated centuries represent a kind of dead weight contributing to a sense of inertia in human affairs? Individuals seem to become more cautious the longer they live. Is not the same true of institutions, such as the church, or of society as a whole? A serious concern with history suggests antiquarianism, a museum mentality that is unresponsive to the future because it seems to be living in the past.

Ever since Henry Ford derided history as "bunk,"[3] many Americans have assumed that progress requires a conscious repudiation of yesterday as a source of challenge for tomorrow.

In our last chapter we saw that Scripture, especially in its climactic New Testament expression, spanned a spectrum from the inherited conservatism of James, who clung to local custom even in the face of impending catastrophe, to the breathtaking liberalism of Stephen, who would have abolished centuries of venerable tradition without a moment's hesitation. But now we must ask whether the biblical spectrum, with all of its built-in freedom and flexibility, has survived twenty centuries of church history. After all, apostolic Christianity was a new thing, in the first flush of missionary enthusiasm, uninhibited by institutional trappings, not yet controlled even by its own canon, creed, or clergy.

What happened to that daring experiment once it became locked in the embrace of the centuries? Was the creative balance that Christianity struck between conservatism and liberalism possible only in the Apostolic Age? Or was the dynamic equilibrium reflected in the New Testament such an integral part of the nascent faith that it could not be destroyed even by the vicissitudes of history?

To answer that crucial question, let us look first at the classical era of church history that stretched from the second to the seventeenth centuries, embracing what are usually called the Patristic, Medieval, and Reformation periods. Then let us turn to the modern era ushered in by the political, intellectual, and religious revolutions of the eighteenth century that have yet to run their course. In this period we shall concentrate on the Baptist experience as it shapes the matrix of our work today.

Needless to say, it will be just as impossible in this chapter to survey the entire sweep of Christian history as it was in the last chapter to survey the entire sweep of Scripture. However, if I am able here to illustrate a way of interrogating and evaluating the evidence, perhaps that will suggest a methodology and provide a framework for your own lifetime of more detailed investigation. For this purpose, I propose to treat one theological development in each of the three periods of the classical era and, moreover, to choose the development that is widely thought to raise the most pivotal issue and to involve the most influential personality of that period. For the Patristic period, I shall consider the Hellenizing of Christianity with special reference to Aurelius Augustine; for the Medieval period, the Aristotelianizing of Christianity with special reference to

Thomas Aquinas; and, for the Reformation period, the existentializing of Christianity with special reference to Martin Luther.

I

Christianity was conceived in a Jewish womb. We remember the epigram of Julius Wellhausen that "Jesus was not a Christian: he was a Jew."[4] The marks of this historical heredity are plain to see in the lives of its founding fathers, the original apostles. But, almost immediately, an outbreak of persecution caused a rupture with the Jewish community that deepened a separate Christian identity. Furthermore, the missionary mandate of the young faith drove it quickly into the Graeco-Roman world, first to the Jewish synagogues but soon to the cosmopolitan Hellenistic masses. From the beginning its Scriptures were the Greek Old Testament (Septuagint), and all of its own writings, which eventually became the New Testament, were also in Greek. But, even more importantly, the church early began to take on Graeco-Roman features in its organizational life, its worship practices, and its theological formulations.

This process of acculturation has been called the Hellenization of Christianity especially since the definitive treatment of the subject by Adolf Harnack, who understood "dogma in its conception and development as a work of the Greek spirit on the soil of the Gospel."[5] The main lines of Christian orthodoxy were established within the first six centuries of church history, and to Harnack, as expounded in his magisterial *History of Dogma*, the major theme in that story was the way in which the very structure of Christian thought was permanently shaped by Greek philosophy. This change represented, in Harnack's view, not merely an addition, or even an adaptation, of the original Jewish framework, but a fundamental alteration of its modality that introduced a significant measure of discontinuity between New Testament theology and ecclesiastical theology. That is why "the attempts at deducing the genesis of the church's doctrinal system from the theology of Paul, or from compromises between Apostolic doctrinal ideas, will always miscarry; for they fail to note that to the most important premises of the Catholic doctrine of faith belongs an element that we cannot recognize as dominant in the New Testament, namely, the Hellenic spirit."[6]

Many examples might be given of the reformulation of biblical concepts in Hellenistic terms, involving basic affirmations about the existence of God, the divinity of Christ, and the nature of the church. Here, the most important thing to note is how much freedom Patristic theologians felt to innovate by utilizing philosophic materials drawn from the pagan world and to abandon salient features of New Testament faith, such as apocalyptic eschatology and charismatic enthusiasm.

In accordance with the working definitions adopted in this study, the development of Patristic theology would have to be evaluated as a decidedly liberal achievement. I realize that the popular stereotype of the "Church Fathers" is conservative and that they have long been appealed to by traditionalists, especially in the Anglican communion, as a court of last resort. But, measured by their tolerance of discontinuity, their responsiveness to new situations, and their willingness to experiment with the central affirmations of the Gospels, these church fathers were theological liberals of the first rank!

Before we conclude, however, that the Patristic period ought to be viewed as a liberal era because of the originality of its doctrines, we need to give attention to an equally important development taking place concurrently with the development of Hellenistic theology, namely, the canonization of the New Testament. Here was an idea that was never even seriously considered until Irenaeus responded to the heretical canon of Marcion late in the second century. Once the possibility of an orthodox canon was conceived, it was slow in being implemented, with definitive lists of approved books not appearing until late in the fourth century. It was as if the church canonized the New Testament out of some inner necessity that could not be denied.

Few subjects are as complex or obscure as the history of the New Testament canon. I need not enter here into detail regarding the books chosen for eventual inclusion or into the motives for their selection. Rather, I invite your attention to the dates when the very idea of having a New Testament canon was fixed in Christian thought. The interesting thing to observe is that these periods of concern for canonicity virtually coincided with the times when the Patristic church was hammering out its distinctive doctrines. The church decided to elevate to canonical status a group of increasingly ancient apostolic writings that expressed the faith primarily in Jewish categories at the same time that it was deciding to elevate to confessional status a group of doctrinal statements that expressed the faith primarily in Greek categories. Nor do we find any evidence that the church felt it was creating a contradiction, or even a conflict, in its theological position by fostering these parallel developments.

If the Hellenization of Patristic doctrine must be viewed as a decidedly liberal venture, the canonization of the New Testament must be viewed as an equally conservative venture. After all, here were documents that spoke of the Kingdom of God, the apostolic kerygma, and the life of the church in ways that were anachronistic in the fourth century AD To be sure, the argument from antiquity was useful in refuting heretics and convincing skeptics, but the church was only creating trouble for itself by conferring sacred status on writings that nowhere authenticated or even encouraged the basic direction in which the church itself was moving. Then why the dogged impulse to have such a canon? Because the church recognized in Christ a reality transcending any context, whether Jewish or Greek, and it determined with sound instinct to conserve those writings, however strange and distant, that mediated to later ages his unique historical ministry in its original impact.

The broad lines of my assessment of Patristic Christianity are now beginning to become clear. In many and varied ways, but especially by its concurrent Hellenization of doctrine and canonization of Scripture, the church was declaring its intention to be both liberal and conservative at the same time. Indeed, an entirely new context for ministry demanded a dual response.

On the one hand, there was no way to engage the Greek mind with the gospel without resorting to terminology and concepts it could understand. Nor was this simply a matter of "translation" as we understand that task today. In the modern world, Western Christianity has a language all its own that roots in a comprehensive culture that missionaries can attempt to transplant—whether wisely or not—into a new setting with a minimum of change. But Apostolic Christianity had been forced to abandon its Judaic culture; thus it entered the Graeco-Roman world with a gospel that needed both a new language and a new culture in order to become indigenous. Patristic "liberalism"—its thoroughgoing Hellenization of the gospel—was not a theological aberration but an evangelistic imperative.

On the other hand, once the church became truly indigenous on Greek soil, it needed some external frame of reference to insure stability and continuity in the midst of a volatile culture that was on the verge of collapse. This fixed criterion it created for itself by canonizing the most approved apostolic writings as New Testament scriptures. To borrow a paradox from Paul, this was Patristic Christianity's way of saying, "We are truly *in*, but not ultimately *of*, the Hellenistic world" (2 Cor. 10:3). The point is: The church acted conservatively in the canonization of the New Testament, not in opposition to liberalism nor in some compromise with liberalism, but precisely because it had acted liberally in the Hellenization of the gospel. These two strategies did not offset or neutralize each other, but rather complemented and reinforced each other.

Proof that both tendencies were prominent in Patristic leaders might be adduced from a study of Tertullian as a conservative and of Origen as a liberal. Rather than adopt that polarizing approach, however, I would prefer to remind you that both tendencies coexisted creatively in the life of Aurelius Augustine, bishop of Hippo, who without question represented the most profound expression and enduring achievement of Patristic Christianity. Augustine is often included in a catalogue of the conservative giants of history because of his pessimistic view of human nature, but his constantly changing life was far too complex for so simple a categorization. He, more than anyone else, grafted Christian doctrine to Neoplatonic thought, that repository of the entire philosophic tradition of Hellenism. For example, Augustine found in Neoplatonism a conception of evil he used not only to refute the Manichees, but also to formulate a Christian doctrine of creation. And yet it was also Augustine who, more than any other Patristic theologian, used the canonical Scriptures to inform and buttress his faith. He took so seriously the Christian canon that he may fairly be called the first great biblical preacher and theologian in anything like the modern sense of those terms.

Proof that Augustine achieved a balance of conservative and liberal perspectives is provided by his most mature work, *The City of God*, an extraordinarily rich source of insight for our study because it was written at a time of great social upheaval when civilization itself seemed threatened to the core. As Peter Brown has brilliantly shown, the key to this profound treatise is found in the concept of Christian existence as *peregrination*, or the status of a "resident alien."[7]

On the one hand, believers are not to be escapists from "this common mortal life,"[8] gloating over the sack of Rome and the impending fall of the Empire. Rather, they are to celebrate the essential goodness of human achievements within the created order as lavish gifts from the hand of God.[9] But, on the other hand, because the devil seeks to usurp the earthly realm for his own evil ends, believers find themselves surrounded by sin and judgment, heightening within them an intense longing for the heavenly city of God. This "homesickness" was anticipated by the exiles in Babylon sighing for release and by the prophets who prefigured the coming of Christ and the age of the church. In the pilgrims and sojourners of each new generation, this yearning for fulfillment nourishes a determination to be otherworldly in a world that they cannot help but love.

For Augustine, Christian conservatism represented a grateful steward-ship of the "given" that can never be treated as second best because it roots in the perfection of the creator God, a goodness that can still be seen and celebrated in the created order despite the corruption caused by Satan. Christian liberalism for Augustine began where his Christian conservatism left off, with the capacity to want something better when confronted with "a life so full of so many and such various evils that it can hardly be called living."[10] His liberalism was both continuous and consis-tent with his conservatism and, indeed, was required for its completion. There is no reason to "conserve" a good but fallen creation unless it will be eventually "liberated."

II

Many Christians have shown little interest in the Medieval period, disdaining it as a thousand-year "Dark Age" (AD 500-1500) whose gloom was dispelled only by the Protestant Reformation. On the contrary, it was a rich and varied era, especially during the thirteenth century, a time of momentous change marking a watershed in Western civilization.

Politically, this was the century of the Magna Carta, the founding of the Hanseatic League, and the emergence of a nationalism that strength-ened the state at the expense of the church. Economically, it was a time of expanding commerce as the Crusades and travels of Marco Polo opened trade routes to the East, as serfdom gave way to an emerging middle class bourgeoisie, and as merchant guilds created new markets in Europe. Culturally, it was the age of Dante, of the Gothic cathedrals, and of the great national traditions that lie at the base of all Western literatures in the vernacular. Intellectually, it was the period when modern universities were founded, when waves of Arabic influence were being mediated from the Islamic world, and when the anti-clerical free thought of secularism challenged theologians for the European mind.

A century of such momentous upheaval provides a splendid setting in which to test the church's response to the crisis of change. Nor could the challenge be avoided. The rediscovery of Aristotle through Arabic scholars in Spain, and the popularization of his thought at the University of Paris by Siger of Brabant, gave students a taste of scientific philosophy congenial to the times that made the Neoplatonic theology of orthodoxy seem suddenly out of date. Ecclesiastical authorities rushed in to forbid instruction in Aristotle, but this only precipitated the first great clash between science and religion. Either the church would learn to Christianize Aristotle—by reason, not by dogma!—or it would lose the best minds of its day. This urgent challenge it began to meet, first through Albert the Great, and then through his even greater student, Thomas Aquinas.

The vast system of thought that Thomas unfolded in his two *Summas* reflected an underlying strategy by which he responded to the ferment of thirteenth-century intellectual life. In the words of A. C. McGiffert:

> . . . Thomas was a modernist and his great effort was to reinterpret the Christian system in the light of Aristotle, or in other words to form a synthesis of Christian theology and Aristotelian philosophy. He was convinced that Aristotelianism had come to stay and was bound in the end to be generally accepted by intelligent men. Christianity, therefore, must make terms with it, so he believed, if it were not to lose the confidence of the educated classes. At the same time he was a devout and orthodox believer and the last thing he wanted was to sacrifice Christian truth to the demands of Aristotelianism or any other philosophy.[11]

Despite the brilliant erudition and gentle spirit of its master, Thomistic philosophy "was received by most of his contemporaries as a monstrous accumulation of pagan reasonings fatal to the Christian faith."[12] The Franciscans, for example, under the leadership of Bonaventura, a lifelong friend and opponent of Thomas, were shocked by its intellectualism, which offended their mystical piety, and by its rejection of Augustinian Platonism. Within three years after Thomas' premature death at age forty-nine, many of his teachings were condemned as heretical by the archbishops both of Paris and of Canterbury. But eventually it became clear to the Church that Thomas had in fact been able to conserve undiminished the substance of Christian truth despite his revolutionary alteration of its form. In 1323 he was canonized by Pope John XXII, in 1567 he was pronounced "the Angelic Doctor" of the church by Pope Pius V, and in 1880 his system of thought was made the basis of instruction in all Catholic schools by Pope Leo XIII.

We have already seen that conservative and liberal instincts may coexist, not only compatibly, but also creatively, within the same life, which was also the case with Thomas. This does not mean, however, that an equal balance of the two tendencies should always be sought as a sort of "golden mean." As we discovered when comparing Stephen and James, the challenge at a given time and place may require either a strongly liberal or a strongly conservative response in order to correct an imbalanced situation.

What church history adds to this picture from the perspective of the centuries is not simply the familiar maxim that the liberalism of one generation is often the conservatism of the next. Rather, it is the realization that a strongly liberal response in a particular situation may be the best way—indeed, may be the *only* way—for conservatives to protect that which is under attack. Conversely, in a quite different situation a strongly conservative response may be the best way for liberals to preserve their most cherished values from destruction. Such role reversals need not represent a compromise of position by the individual, for integrity is well understood as consistent intentionality in response to the necessities of history.

III

Of all the periods of classical Christianity, none is of greater interest to Protestants than the Reformation, with its dominant figure, Martin Luther. And yet no leader in Christian history is more difficult to classify in terms of our present inquiry. On the one hand, Luther was surely the most conservative Christian who ever lived. His mind and heart were captive to the Word of God. In fidelity to that absolute norm he did not flinch from sweeping away centuries of accretions embodied in the papacy, the Mass, and the system of indulgences. Nor did he do this as an iconoclast but as one determined to take historic Catholicism more seriously than the Roman Catholic Church!

Yet, on the other hand, Luther was surely the most liberal Christian who ever lived. For he dared to put his solitary convictions above the collective consensus of the church and to follow the logic of those convictions wherever they might lead. Unlike Aquinas, whose elaborate philosophy he repudiated, Luther did not reach *backward* to Aristotle for an ancient structure of thought with which to support his faith. Rather, he reached *inward* to rest faith on an existential commitment and, in so doing, helped launch the modern era.

Beyond Luther himself, what was the meaning of the Reformation itself for the nature of the church? No one has pondered this issue more carefully than the premier scholar of the Lutheran Reformation, Jaroslav Pelikan, who answered in terms borrowed from Paul Tillich[13]: "Catholic substance and Protestant principle."[14] By the former he meant the heritage of ancient tradition, liturgy, and dogma that the leaders of the Reformation were determined to preserve even if excommunicated as "holy apostates." By the latter he meant the critical reverence toward the inherited "given" in order to reconstruct it in the name of the gospel and by the authority of the Bible. In other words, the sixteenth-century Reformation paradigm was, by its very nature, both conservative and liberal. It gathered up into one unified perspective the need to preserve and the need to purge, the task of constructing and the task of criticizing. In this dialectic lies the unfinished reformation that makes obedient rebels or conservative liberals of us all. Rather than documenting that in the life of Luther, let us face its impact on the Baptists since they have been in a recent struggle over how to implement these Reformation principles.

IV

The European Reformation of the sixteenth century sent out shock waves leading to the English Reformation of the seventeenth century that had far more direct influence on the development of Baptists than did the former. Students of history will remember that the Church of England was separated from the Church of Rome by the Act of Supremacy in 1534 during the reign of Henry VIII. However, much of Roman Catholic form and substance remained even after an aggressive effort at reform under Edward VI.

When England returned to Romanism under Queen Mary in 1553, many Protestant leaders who escaped martyrdom fled to the Continent, where they found a far more thoroughgoing reformation already underway in centers such as Geneva. The return of Protestantism to the British throne with the beginning of Queen Elizabeth's reign in 1558 gave great hopes to these exiles, causing many of them to return to their homeland with visions of a Calvinistic commonwealth on British soil.

Alas, their dreams were at least partly thwarted by the determination of Elizabeth to remain firmly in control of the Church of England, leading to three developments of great relevance to our study. First, those who were dissatisfied with the modest reforms early in Elizabeth's reign, and were determined to rid the Church of England of the last vestiges of "popery," gradually organized themselves after 1575 into "Puritans," concerned for the "purity" of Christianity in personal, congregational, and national life.

Second, some of these Puritans, frustrated by long delays and meager results in reforming the established church, rejected the strategy of compromise with the Crown, repudiated the established church, and became Separatists—sometimes called Independents, Dissenters, or Nonconformists—who organized themselves into voluntary congregations covenanted to put into practice, without delay, the Puritan marks of the true church.

Third, bitterly persecuted as sectarians, some of these Separatists began to seek asylum in Holland where they were influenced by Mennonites of the Radical Reformation in Europe. One such group from Lincolnshire, under the leadership of John Smyth, came to accept the New Testament practice of believer's baptism, which it applied to thirty-seven of its number in 1609, thereby becoming the first of what may properly be called Baptist churches in the historical sense of that term.

Although too much weight should not be attached to the circumstances surrounding one's origin, it is only accurate to say that the birth of the Baptist denomination represented a powerful expression of the reformation principle. The oft-debated question of whether Baptists are "Protestants" is truly ambiguous, not because of the secessionist theories advanced in opposition to such an identification, but because Baptists were not a part of the original Reformation but rather sprang from efforts to reform that Reformation. They arose, not in protest against Catholicism, but in protest against an incomplete Protestantism! In terms of our conservative-liberal spectrum, clearly the shifts from Establishmentarianism to Puritanism, then from Puritanism to Separatism, then from Separatism to Anabaptism, were all movements leftward. Indeed, Michael Walzer has found in the English Calvinism energizing this entire "revolution of the saints" the earliest forms of the political radicalism that gave rise to the modern state.[15]

Without a doubt, the initial impulse that gave rise to the Baptists was liberal in character, not only in the formal ideological sense of insistence on change in established institutions, but also in the historical sense of direct ties to those political activities that nourished the roots of classical English liberalism. And yet, the original Baptist impulse was also profoundly conservative, representing a repristinization that determined to recover the spirit and practices of the earliest New Testament churches. In other words, here again was the same kind of situation that we had occasion to notice in our evaluation of Thomas Aquinas, one in which the only way to conserve the *normative past* was to rebel against the *traditional past*. It was in the genius of this impulse that it risked complete discontinuity with the established church in order to forge a forgotten continuity with the New Testament church.

The subsequent Baptist experience in America highlights yet another facet of our complex subject. At first, the liberal impulse of non-conforming dissent came through strongly, such as in the 1639 banishment of Roger Williams from the Massachusetts Bay Colony and in the public whippings and jailings throughout the colonial period for refusal to support the established church. But with the triumph of liberal democracy over the last vestiges of conservative aristocracy, Baptists began to flourish so much that, by the end of the nineteenth century, they had become part of a new religious establishment, especially in many parts of the South.

With the reversal of social roles among Baptists came a new mood of reactionary conservatism, nourished in part by the feudalistic mentality of slave-holding landowners and even more by the regional trauma of crushing defeat in the Civil War. This drift toward the Right was further accelerated after World War II, especially when the liberal Democratic Party under Lyndon Johnson led in abolishing segregation, throwing most Southern Baptists into the conservative Republican Party of Ronald Reagan.

There is, of course, deep irony in these developments that we cannot turn aside to explore. The point is: Conservatism and liberalism are not only reflections of one's personal temperament or convictions, but are also a reflection of one's social situation and historical frame of reference. The perspective of a hunted heretic is not that of his orthodox inquisitor, nor is the attitude of a conscientious objector in jail that of his well-respected jailor. Baptists have not clung to one spot on the ideological spectrum through the centuries as if it were somehow theologically superior to those occupied by other denominations. Rather, they have moved from one end of the spectrum to the other because they have been responsive to the challenges and influences of each new socio-historical situation, which situations have changed drastically, particularly in America.

To return to a question raised early in this chapter: Has the church through its long history been able to maintain that dynamic equilibrium between conservatism and liberalism so creatively exemplified in Holy Scripture? The answer to these brief probings would have to be in the affirmative. Such a conclusion does not suggest that each era or each individual leader held these two tendencies in some sort of quantitative balance at every time and place. But it does suggest that the deepest instinct of the Christian faith is to "fine tune" the process of change so that it will conserve that which is normative from the past while liberating that which is needed for the future.

Our next task will be to ask why this is so: Why does church history, taken as a whole, resemble an ellipse formed by the two foci of Catholic fidelity and Protestant flux? Why does Baptist history, taken as a whole, run the gamut from a people responding as liberals in a conservative environment to the same people responding as conservatives in a liberal environment?

The answer must be that there is something inherent within the Christian faith that contributes to this overriding characteristic of church history. In other words, the controlling realities of Christian theology must speak directly to the dialectic of conservatism and liberalism. How and why this is so will be the subject of our next chapter.

Notes

[1]Will and Ariel Durant, *The Story of Civilization*, 11 vols. (New York: Simon and Schuster, 1935-75).

[2]Will and Ariel Durant, *The Lessons of History* (New York: Simon and Schuster, 1968), 35-36.

[3]Henry Ford, in an interview with Charles N. Wheeler of the *Chicago Tribune* on May 25, 1916, said, "History is more or less bunk."

[4]Julius Wellhausen, *Einleitung in die ersten Evangelien* (Berlin: Reimer, 1905), 113; discussed in context by Joseph Klausner, *Jesus of Nazareth* (London: George Allen & Unwin, 1925), 95.

[5]Adolph Harnack, *History of Dogma*, 1 (Boston: Roberts, 1897), 17, 21-22.

[6]Ibid., 48-49.

[7]Peter Brown, *Augustine of Hippo: A Biography*, 312-329 on "Civitas Peregrina."

[8]Augustine, *The City of God*, XV, 21, 15.

[9]Ibid., XIX, 13, 57-75.

[10]Ibid., XXII, 22, 1.

[11]Arthur Cushman McGiffert, *A History of Christian Thought*, 2 (New York: Charles Scribner's Sons, 1933), 259-260.

[12]Will Durant, *The Age of Faith* (New York: Simon and Schuster, 1980), 977.

[13]Paul Tillich, *The Protestant Era* (Chicago: University of Chicago Press, 1948), esp. ix-xxix, 161-181; *Systematic Theology*, vol. 3 (Chicago: University of Chicago Press, 1963), esp. 243-245.

[14]Jaroslav Pelikan, *Obedient Rebels: Catholic Substance and Protestant Principle in Luther's Reformation* (New York: Harper & Row, 1964).

[15]Michael Walzer, *The Revolution of the Saints: A Study in the Origins of Radical Politics* (Cambridge: Harvard University Press, 1965).

CHAPTER 4

A Theological Critique
of Conservatism and Liberalism

We come here to the final stage of our methodology for a Christian understanding of conservatism and liberalism. Findings from three thousand years of biblical and church history suggest that, in each new situation, our faith has deliberately sought to strike a balance between tradition and innovation that honors the values both of continuity and of change. This bipolar commitment to the claims of antiquity and of modernity results in a creative tension we have called "dynamic equilibrium," a characteristic of Christianity too deliberate and recurring to be accidental. It is as if the gospel has a built-in gyroscope that "fine tunes" its responsiveness in the present to both past and future on the long trajectory through history.

This phenomenon encourages us to investigate our faith in its definitive form to determine whether there is something inherent in Christian doctrine that accounts for this distinctive attitude toward time. If theology be understood as an effort to talk intelligibly about the nature of ultimate reality, then this critique must probe the very structure and substance of Christian affirmation to discover whether, and to what extent, it is compatible with those constructs of human existence that supply the presuppositions of conservatism and liberalism. Both of these ideologies arose outside of a religious setting and did not presume to call themselves "theology" at all, being content to function in the more limited role of a political or economic outlook. Recently, however, as we saw in the first chapter, many religionists have sought to baptize one or the other of these viewpoints as a normative theological category, thus making the critique on which we now embark both appropriate and important.

I

In the judgment of many people, the greatest single theological clarification of the twentieth century was the recognition that Christianity is a profoundly eschatological religion. That is, at its deepest level, our faith originally understood itself as the gathering of a new people of God for a new age of human history that, as the "last times," represented the climactic epoch in God's dealings with creation. Because this understanding was first formed in a Jewish setting, it was largely obscured as Christianity shifted to a Hellenistic environment. For centuries, eschatology was treated as a concluding subject on the afterlife rather than as the conceptual framework for all doctrine. However, the development of a critical historiography in the nineteenth century set the stage for a rediscovery of the primacy of eschatology in the twentieth century.

German theologians were in the forefront of efforts to recover this forgotten framework of our faith. Based on a fresh study of inter-testamental Jewish apocalyptic literature, scholars such as Johannes Weiss and Albert Schweitzer startled their contemporaries at the turn of the century with the hypothesis that Jesus and his followers expected the imminent end of the world. Indeed, Schweitzer's *Quest of the Historical Jesus* may be taken as the manifesto of this interpretation, which is often called "futuristic" or "thoroughgoing" or "consistent" eschatology (*Konsequent Eschatologie*). These descriptive labels, which suffer in English translation from the German, refer to a far more important issue than chronological calculations regarding the nearness of the end. They assert that Jesus was dominated by futurity, that he saw all continuities in a state of near collapse, that he interpreted each present moment as a provisional "interim" already conditioned by catastrophic change that would soon come. The overriding passion of Jesus was to prepare for the end, indeed, to hasten its coming. This was the central reality with which his disciples had to deal in redefining their faith after the eschaton failed to materialize.

This one-sided understanding of eschatology from Germany was soon answered by its opposite side from Great Britain, most notably through the writings of C. H. Dodd, especially in *The Parables of the Kingdom* and soon thereafter in *The Apostolic Preaching and Its Developments*. Dodd argued that the dominant conviction of Jesus was that the long-awaited kingdom of God had actually arrived in his ministry, a position that came to be called "realized eschatology." Again, the issue was not timetable as such but a more fundamental temporal orientation. If Dodd was correct, then Jesus understood his religion primarily in terms of what had *already* happened "since the days of John the Baptist" (Matt. 11:12) rather than in terms of what was *yet* to happen "when the Son of Man comes"

(Matt. 10:23). For his followers after his departure, this conviction would shift their religious center of gravity from the future to the past, from parousia to incarnation, from a mood of anticipation to one of fulfillment.

The longer we ponder the evidence for both of these brilliantly argued but ultimately incompatible views, the more clearly we realize that both positions contain a measure of truth. Therefore, it should not be surprising to find that scholars such as Joachim Jeremias and W. G. Kümmel advanced a mediating view, often called "inaugurated" or "proleptic" eschatology to render a German phase (*sich realisierende Eschatologie*) that I would translate as "eschatology becoming actualized." This position implied that the decisive event had already taken place in the past but its full consummation was yet awaited in the future. Another way of putting it is to say that, for Jesus and his church, the eschaton had entered into time but could not yet be fully implemented within human history.

What we are being driven to accept by the force of evidence from both sides is a recognition that there is a paradoxical element in Christian eschatology. Unlike its Jewish antecedents, it affirms that the new age of the Messiah not only can but did invade the old age of sin and death *without thereby abolishing it.* To borrow from the Apostle Paul, this means that we live where the ages impinge and overlap (1 Cor. 10:11). In such a situation, one must take with equal seriousness a past in which decisive changes have already occurred and a future in which equally decisive changes will yet occur. Stated simply, the dialectical character of Christian eschatology, which determines the very nature of our theology, demands that we take with the utmost seriousness both past and future, and thereby that we be both conservative and liberal at the same time.

II

This analysis of eschatology has prepared us for a second line of inquiry that concerns Christology. In Judaism, messianic expectations were but one aspect of a larger future hope when the Messiah might play a major or minor role. In Christianity, however, the person and work of Jesus invested messianic categories with such significance that christological doctrine came to stand on its own as a major focus of affirmation. This carried the attendant danger that it could be divorced from those eschatological assumptions necessary for an understanding of its meaning. For example, Christology formulated on Greek philosophical premises succumbed to that danger. We shall try to overcome such distortions by setting Christology once again in its original Jewish eschatological context.

When we ask how early Christians related Jesus of Nazareth to Jewish messianic thought, two answers are immediately obvious. First, they began by designating Jesus as "the Christ." While we take this identification for granted, such a connection was not that axiomatic in the first-century situation. After all, Jesus had been extremely reticent in applying Jewish christological categories to his own ministry (Mark 8:30). Furthermore, he had been rejected as Messiah by the highest Jewish tribunal, which presumably was competent to judge his credentials on this point (Mark 14:61-64). Finally, this would be an embarrassing title to take into the Hellenistic world at a time when Jewish messianism was suspected of fomenting insurrection against Rome.

Despite these formidable problems, early Christians chose instead to identify their Master closely with the Jewish Messiah. This title, which had always been used functionally of an office, quickly became in its Greek form a part of his proper name: "Jesus Christ." Why was not a more universal, exalted title substituted for this ambiguous, provincial epithet? Because his followers knew that the life and work of Jesus could not be adequately understood apart from his Jewish rootage. In a very real sense, they stamped his ministry with the scandal of particularity when they branded him as "Jesus *the Christ.*" It was the most conservative thing they could have done, because it forever linked him to his own people in their most particularistic expression.

And yet they did a second thing that moved in the opposite direction. Judaism had always envisioned that the Messiah would come only at the end of history, never in its middle. But the early Christians immediately divided this expectation into two parts, holding that their Messiah had come already in hidden lowliness and that he would come again in heavenly splendor. In so doing, they split Christology into past and future tenses, which has remained its essential structure to this day. But notice that they made this daring shift without any scriptural encouragement from the Old Testament. At the very moment when the early church was doing something very conservative in designating Jesus as "the Christ," they were also doing something very liberal in describing his messiahship as having both past and future dimensions.

This fundamental alteration of Christology has profound implications for our understanding of the proper relationship between conservatism and liberalism. On the one hand, by viewing the earthly ministry of Jesus as an eschatological event, we thereby invest a particular piece of history with an ultimacy that no history has ever had before. In the brief and tragic career of an itinerant Galilean preacher, we dare to claim that the Kingdom of God was present (Luke 17:21), that the eternal Word of God was enfleshed (John 1:14), that the redemption of mankind was completed (John 19:30). This means that everything that can be known about the historical Jesus must be "conserved," which explains why the early church included all four of its accepted Gospels in the canon despite the problems raised by their divergent approaches. Salvation history was given a new midpoint that forever defines the normative content of our faith regardless of how much longer time shall last. There simply cannot be a more conservative position than that!

At the same time, Christology compels us to assign as much significance to the final coming of Christ as we do to his first coming. But there is a difference between the two advents that must not be overlooked. The first was in the shame of rejection; the final will be in the glory of vindication. Already the crucified Servant has been exalted to the right hand of the Father in glory where he will reign until every enemy is subdued (1 Cor. 15:25). But only in his parousia will the cosmic sweep of that victory be revealed and the universe be brought to its knees (Phil. 2:9-11). Meanwhile, the verdict is not in doubt because the power of his indwelling Spirit is a guarantee of eventual triumph. Therefore, Christians live in the certainty that the final coming will bring to completion all that was begun in the first century.

This hope asserts that Christ is totally sovereign over the future. In other words, he not only *can* but *will* finally change everything on the face of the earth, destroying all that opposes his cause (1 Cor. 15:24) and perfecting all that embraces his cause (1 Cor. 13:10). Moreover, he will complete this transformation at his Father's good pleasure (Mark 13:32), which means that nothing in history, however firmly fixed and seemingly impervious to change, can stay his hand. With a faith such as this, Christians face the future unafraid either that it will undermine what Christ has already done or that Christ will be unable to break the stranglehold of forces contrary to his cause in the future. The always imminent parousia means that we live in confidence regarding the redeemability of the future. There simply cannot be a more liberal position than that!

What we have learned in this discussion is that when Christology was developed in the context of early Christian eschatology, the bipolar character of the latter caused the former to assign ultimate meaning to those two fixed points that forever define the new age of salvation history: the first coming of Christ in the past and his final coming in the future. The conviction that our lives are set down in the midst of one unfinished christological event, now two thousand years in the making, has the effect not only of defining a distinctive Christian conservatism and liberalism, but also of setting these two orientations in proper balance. On the one hand, we work to "conserve" everything that came to us as a result of Christ's earthly ministry and its subsequent impact through the centuries. On the other hand, we work to "liberate" everything now in bondage that will one day be set free by his glorious return. And because it is "this same Jesus" who both came and will come again (Acts 1:11), we work as conservatives and liberals at the same time!

III

Having considered eschatology and Christology, we turn now to a few remarks on pneumatology, or the doctrine of the Holy Spirit. Our particular angle of approach to so vast a subject is determined by the insights just gleaned from reflecting on Christology. In setting the first and final comings of our Lord as outer limits to the new age of messianic fulfillment, the New Testament provided us with a more spacious temporal orientation than it may have realized. During the early days of the faith, it seemed as if Jesus had just come; indeed, there were still eyewitnesses around who had seen him in the flesh. Likewise, it seemed that his final manifestation might occur at any moment, surely before all of those who had been with him on earth tasted death (Mark 9:1). By contrast, we now look back almost two thousand years to his first coming, which inclines some to look at least that far into the future for his final coming. Ours is hardly the one-generation perspective that greets us in the New Testament (1 Thess. 4:17).

As a result of this shift in temporal perspective from a few years to many centuries, we are left with strong convictions about a rather remote event in the distant past, and about what may prove to be an equally remote event in the distant future. But what about our attitudes toward the immediate past and the immediate future? This, in fact, is where the rub often comes as regards our primary agenda. Those who talk most loudly about conservatism often have in mind little more than preserving some feature of contemporary life that may have been in existence for forty or fifty years, while those who match their noise level in commending liberalism often advocate some fad that will do well to last for another forty or fifty years into the future. As challenging as it would be to grapple with more enduring issues, we must face the fact that forty or fifty years in both directions covers the entire life span that any of us is given to enjoy and thus defines the widest temporal limits with which many people will ever be concerned.

Fortunately, early Christianity was keenly interested in the problem of what to retain and what to reject in each new situation, especially because vigorous missionary expansion, combined with turbulent social conditions, required the movement to interact with a rapidly changing world. The Gospel of John, in particular, sought to recast material regarding the Jewish Jesus of Palestine to meet the mindset of Greeks influenced by a host of Hellenistic ideas. Because we can compare the Fourth Gospel with the Synoptics, we are in a position to realize that, in fulfilling this assignment, the author made more sweeping changes in order to get his message ready for the future than did any other book in the New Testament, but without thereby destroying its continuity with the past.

Because the Fourth Evangelist made such a daring adaptation of tradition by and about Jesus at a time when the synoptic alternative was already well established, he felt constrained to include some explanation and justification for his finished product within the Gospel itself. This he did by attributing to the work of the Holy Spirit the creative freedom that he was able to exercise in responding to a new situation. Although there are hints of this process at work throughout the book (John 2:22, 12:16, 13:7, 16:22-25), its explicit rationale comes to clearest expression in the five Paraclete sayings of John 14-16, the last of which speaks so directly to our agenda that it may be quoted in full:

> I still have many things to say to you, but you cannot bear them now. When the Spirit of truth comes, he will guide you into all the truth; for he will not speak on his own, but will speak whatever he hears, and he will declare to you the things that are to come. He will glorify me, because he will take what is mine and declare

> it to you. All that the Father has is mine. For this reason
> I said that he will take what is mine and declare it to
> you. (John 16:12-15)

Notice the deliberate balance in this passage between two dialectical emphases. On the one hand, the dependence of the Spirit upon Christ is heavily underscored. The only truth given the Paraclete to declare is that which he first receives from Christ (vv. 14b, 15b) by listening to him (v. 13a). This passive role is dictated by two premises: first, that the Father has entrusted the totality of his truth to the Son (v. 15a); and, second, that the Son has been faithful to reveal everything that he was given by the Father (15:15). Therefore, the Spirit has no independent authority to reveal anything on his own (v. 13b).

Perhaps there were those in the Johannine community who, caught up in prophetic inspiration or charismatic enthusiasm, sought to claim the Spirit's sanction for pronouncements that would supercede the revelation given by the historical Jesus. But the Fourth Evangelist would not countenance any embellishment of the Gospel. Such voices were not the Spirit speaking, for his only source of truth is in Christ alone. There could not be a more conservative doctrine of the Holy Spirit in any religion!

But, on the other hand, this same passage puts sharp limits on the ability of the earthly Jesus to declare his full revelation to the disciples, due not to any deficiency on his part but to their inability to bear it (v. 12). The obtuseness of the disciples in understanding their Master is a major motif in this and other Gospels: witness the next paragraph in John where they lament, "We do not know what he means" (v. 18).

In reply, Jesus could only promise that in the future they would understand and therefore question him no more (vv. 23, 25). It is only when the Paraclete "comes" that the disciples may enter into a new relationship with him made possible by the departure of Jesus, that they will be guided into all truth to include a disclosure of coming events (v. 13). The claim being made here is that the future is like a journey on which believers have a guide, one who will, along the way, help them both to comprehend what has already happened and to anticipate what is yet to happen, and so lead them to their final destination where they will discover "all truth." There could not be a more liberal doctrine of the Holy Spirit in any religion!

Again, conservatism and liberalism are not set in opposition, nor is each somehow diluted or compromised by the other as if they were mutually incompatible. Rather, they both stand side by side in full strength, as it were, and yet in perfect balance. In this passage, the two emphases alternate verse by verse, almost phrase by phrase, as if they are two sides of a single coin. Any impartial theologian would have to admit that both past and future are given their full due, that the claims both of continuity and of change are fully honored. The truth yet to come will be both new and yet the same, just as the Gospel of John was new in comparison with the Synoptics, yet the same as them in presenting Jesus Christ as Savior and Lord (20:31). As Rudolph Schnackenburg put it, "Through the Paraclete, the whole Church is intimately connected with the revelation of Jesus Christ and at the same time taken beyond it in so far as new insights and decisions are required by changing historical situations."[1]

It is here that we find the answer to our quest for a "one generation" perspective, similar to that in the New Testament, regarding conservatism and liberalism. Although eschatology and Christology give ultimate meaning to both past and future in terms of the first and final comings of Christ, pneumatology gives existential meaning to these temporal dimensions by defining the work of the Holy Spirit as that of "bringing to our remembrance" all that Jesus revealed in the days of his flesh (John 14:26) and of "declaring to us the things that are to come" until that revelation is perfectly understood as "all truth" (John 16:13). The impact of the Spirit's "coming" into our lives is in effect an eschatological event here and now, taking a seemingly remote incarnation and a seemingly remote parousia and *bringing them both near*, making their meaning a vital part of our own generation, allowing us to live in bipolar fashion on the foundation of Christ's first advent and on the frontier of his final advent. Through the indwelling Spirit, the character of every present moment is shaped by the impact of the first coming in our immediate past and the impact of the final coming in our immediate future.

Therefore, each moment is a challenge both to remember Christ as the ultimate source of divine truth and to interpret that truth in ways that are relevant to our specific situation. The source *never* changes; the situation *always* changes. Because fixed content and fluid context are always set in the sharpest juxtaposition, we must ever be conservative about the substance of our faith and yet liberal about its shape. It is precisely here, on the ever-moving line between past and future, that "dynamic equilibrium" has meaning. Only one who has taken the necessity for continuity with seriousness should be allowed to experiment with change. Conversely, only one who has taken the necessity for change with seriousness should be entrusted with continuity. Which is only a way of saying that one should not attempt to be either a true conservative or a true liberal without first appreciating and affirming the importance of the other.

IV

Our emphasis in this chapter has been on the centrality of eschatology as seen in both Christology and pneumatology. But one feature of biblical eschatology has not been given sufficient attention. I refer to its correlation with protology, or the doctrine of first things.

Fundamental to Christian eschatology is the biblical doctrine of God as both creator and redeemer. Because the same Lord begins and ends this universe, there is an integral connection between "first things" and "last things" that may be variously expressed in terms of: (1) analogy or parallelism, creation/new creation; (2) contrast or restitution, first Adam/last Adam; (3) superiority or transformation, physical body/spiritual body; and (4) hiddenness or delay, according to which some things created at the beginning are kept in reserve for disclosure at the end such as the celestial temple. Notions of pre-existence and of predestination may have arisen originally in the context of efforts to assert the unity and universality of God's first and final work. This same fusion of protology and eschatology when applied to Christology gave rise to the concept of Christ as "the Alpha and the Omega, the first and the last, the beginning and the end" (Rev. 22:13; see 1:17, 2:8).

This biblical tendency to connect primal time with terminal time was part of a much larger pattern in pre-scientific societies by which mankind sought to break out of the trap of transitoriness by relating life to that which is primordial. In such cultures, events had no intrinsic value within themselves; rather, they acquired value by participating in archetypal realities that transcended them. In some religions, such as of the Greeks and the Babylonians, this effort to escape historical provinciality took the form of a periodic return of the end to the beginning in a cycle of recurring epochs. In the Bible, however, cyclical views of history were never allowed to prevail because of the strong sense of a purposive God guiding the affairs of earth in linear time to their intended consummation.

The alpha and omega of history were not viewed as historical events in the same sense as secular history, or even as saving history, unfolding between their boundaries. They were not fixed points at either end of a timeline, thereby removed from all that went on in-between. Rather, they were beyond history in a human sense, and thus universal in scope. Both creation and consummation were presented in the Bible not as self-contained periods on the outer edges of history, but as continuing processes that permeated all of history. In each new moment of unfolding time, Paradise was being lost and regained somewhere in human experience, not because history was cyclical, but because the God who made Paradise in the first place, and will redeem it from Adam's curse in the last place, was forever working on that task from the beginning of time until its end. This was seen most clearly at the "midpoint" of history in the ministry of Jesus, when creation and consummation, if viewed chronologically, would have been at their most remote but were, in fact, so near as to be united in his saving work.

The relevance of this biblical viewpoint for our contemporary concern with conservatism and liberalism is immediately obvious. On the one hand, the connotations of "creation" suggest many of the ultimate values undergirding conservatism: antiquity, preservation, givenness, concreteness, stability, realism, structure, order, being. On the other hand, the connotations of "consummation" suggest many of the ultimate underpinnings of liberalism: change, innovation, originality, idealism, hope, freedom, equality, universality, becoming.

So what does it mean to affirm, if I may take a text from the Apostolic Fathers, "Behold, I make the last things like the first" (Barnabas 6:13)? Does it not mean that God will finally merge our divergent temporal perspectives, and the ideologies on which they are based, into one unified horizon embracing the whole of human history? Does it not mean that God has, in fact, already done just that in Jesus of Nazareth, who is both alpha and omega although he lived only for a moment at the midpoint of time? Does it not mean that, in Christ, we may strive to contemplate history *sub specie aeternitatis* and thereby, as Baron Fredrich von Hügel said of the Fourth Gospel, "englobe the successiveness of man in the simultaneity of God"?[2]

If these surmises are in any sense correct, then we may now be prepared to return to the enduring issue raised at the beginning of our study, namely the issue of constancy and change as defined by the ancient

Greek philosophers, Parmenides and Heraclitus. You may remember that Parmenides saw the world as a closed system in which change must ultimately be illusory because "what is" cannot come from or pass into nothingness since "nothing," by definition, does not exist. His was a system of radical conservatism rooted in the nature of "being" as stable.

Heraclitus, on the other hand, saw change as the essence of reality, an interaction of opposites being essential to the balance of nature. At bottom, his was a system of radical liberalism rooted in the nature of "becoming" as mutable. The three chapters devoted to a Christian critique found us searching for insights that would resolve the tension created by these philosophical alternatives.

What we have discovered is that Christian theology views human existence from both of these perspectives. "From below," as it were, history is seen as an ever-changing timeline defined by that profound biblical phrase, "And it came to pass . . ." Within the historical continuum, everything is in flux; hence every moment is utterly new. But "from above," as it were, history is seen as moving to where it came from in the beginning, so that, when *everything* has changed, when the totality of human freedom has been honored, then *nothing* will have changed; that is, then the totality of divine sovereignty will have been honored. Ultimately, therefore, we cannot choose between conservatism or liberalism because we cannot choose between creation and consummation, between alpha and omega, between protology and eschatology *because they will finally be the same!*

Notes

[1] Rudolf Schnackenburg, *The Gospel According to St. John*, 3 (New York: Crossroad, 1982), 136.

[2] Friedrich von Hügel, "Gospel of St. John," *Encyclopaedia Britannica*, 13 (Chicago: Encyclopaedia Britannica, 1953): 96.

CHAPTER 5

Applying Conservatism and Liberalism: Case Studies

T
he clear and consistent conclusion based on the relevant biblical, historical, and theological evidence is that Christianity is both conservative and liberal, without any tension between them. It asks its adherents to live out of a Hebrew Bible 3,000 years old and a Greek Bible 2,000 years old. What could be more conservative than that? But when they do, they discover a revolutionary agenda that they are to live out in the twenty-first century. What could be more liberal than that?

There is no better way to test both the validity and the applicability of these findings than to do case studies. I offer two, one biblical and the other contemporary.

I

The Book of Acts features five leaders of the early church, each representing a different position as regards conservatism and liberalism.

1. James was a consistent conservative in his role as leader of the Jerusalem church, defending the right of Jewish Christians to remain entirely within their hereditary culture (Acts 12:17, Gal. 2:9-10).
2. Peter was a mediator on the conservative side, contending for the full acceptance of Gentiles with Jews without requiring that Jews relinquish any of their religious practices (Acts 11:17, Gal. 2:7).
3. Barnabas was a centrist, seeking common ground by equally affirming both the conservative and the liberal practices of the early church (Acts 11:22-24, 13:1-2, 15:36-39; Gal. 2:1-3).
4. Paul was a mediator on the liberal side, contending for the full acceptance of Gentiles with Jews without requiring that Gentiles conform to any Jewish religious practices (Acts 9:15).
5. Stephen was a consistent liberal calling for a daring reading of Scripture supporting the transformation of the Jerusalem Temple (Acts 6:11-14, 7:48-53).

As seen from this listing, the key issue facing the early church was what religious practices of Judaism would be required of its Gentile converts, such as temple worship (Acts 6:13), kosher foods (Gal. 2:12), and the observance of Jewish festivals (Gal. 4:10). By far the most troublesome problem was circumcision, both because the rite was repulsive to many Gentiles and because it had taken on an increasingly subversive political connotation against Rome.

The dispute over circumcision became even more serious because an extremist group within the church was aggressively trying to convince Gentile converts that they must be circumcised (Acts 11:2; 15:1, 5, 24). So a special conference was convened in Jerusalem to settle the matter decisively (Acts 15:6-29). All of the leaders were present except for the martyr Stephen, and they dominated the proceedings. Despite their differences, all four agreed that circumcision was not mandatory for Gentiles. An apostolic letter advocating the tolerance of Jewish religious practices was drafted, and the conference adjourned with things almost as they were before it convened.

In light of this climactic effort by all the leaders of the early church, it is surprising to see how ineffective their solution was. The plan of James to protect Paul in Jerusalem collapsed (Acts 21:17-24). After Peter went to a vague "another place" (Acts 12:17) he was never heard from in his new ministry. Barnabas broke with Paul over John Mark (Acts 15:36-40), suggesting that their young assistant was responsive to pressures in Jerusalem (Acts 13:13) that Paul opposed. When Paul himself next went to Jerusalem, it was widely viewed as a suicide mission (Acts 21:1-14)—which came close to happening when he was almost lynched in the shadow of the sanctuary (Acts 21:27-36).

Acts is telling us that it is very hard for leaders to cross category boundaries. Veterans lost their leadership over a single conservative issue: circumcision. But by daring to universalize a Jewish offspring religion, that courageous act forever defined the nature and mission of the Christian faith as a religion for the whole world.

II

The years of my ministry provide a good example of the impact of the culture on conservatism and liberalism in Christianity. I began to preach in the aftermath of World War II when the United States and its allies had defeated both the Axis powers in Europe and Japan in the Orient. As millions of soldiers returned to complete their education, establish their families and launch their careers, a religious revival filled the churches. Culturally, it was an expansive time that came to a climax in the Camelot years of John F. Kennedy's presidency. Southern Baptists responded by setting ambitious goals for growth and by changing the denominational structure to accommodate it. Hope was in the air. It was a liberal moment.

But with the assassins' bullets the mood began to change. The presumption of continuing progress was rudely shattered by a "decade of shocks" stretching from the assassination of JFK in 1963 to the abdication of Richard M. Nixon as president in 1974.[1] Suddenly an encroaching chaos became part of everyday life, namely:

- the slayings of Robert F. Kennedy and Martin Luther King Jr.
- the collapse of Lyndon Johnson's Great Society and War on Poverty in the jungles of Vietnam
- burning racial ghettos in cities such as Los Angeles and Detroit
- assaults and arrests in droves of civil rights advocates
- campus riots at elite universities from Berkeley to Harvard
- Cold War stalemate following nuclear confrontation in Cuba
- a sexual revolution that undermined the traditional family
- a Watergate burglary that imperiled the U.S. presidency

Suffice it to say that the American dream was in utter disarray. A few avant-garde theologians found religion so impotent to combat these devastating developments that they boldly pronounced God—at least the God enjoyed so much in the 1950s—to be dead![2]

The dominant reaction to this massive destabilization that seemed to assault our most cherished values was one of fear, a complex emotion compounded of frustration over unanticipated failures, fretfulness over an uncertain course of action, and foreboding that the worst was yet to come. It was not just the rapid rate of change that prompted an upsurge of anxiety in the late 1960s and 1970s but the fact that most of these changes were unexpected, unwelcome, and seemingly uncontrollable. The South, in particular, permitted its fears to be exploited by those seeking to attract popular support.

Consider, in particular, the 1968 presidential campaign of George C. Wallace. Running as an independent, the former governor of Alabama spoke to and for "the average man on the street": blue collar workers, small business operators, and farmers—the common people disdained by "all those over-educated ivory-tower folks with pointy heads looking down their noses at us." To those fearful of federal intrusiveness, he promised defiance at the schoolhouse door. To those fuming over Vietnam draft-dodgers, he advocated a patriotism of victory at any cost, selecting as his running mate Gen. Curtis Lemay who famously favored bombing the Communists back to the Stone Age.

Whether it be the upsurge of immorality, the decline of the work ethic, or the disrespect for authority, the antidote was the recovery of traditional morality. The Dixie crowds that roared at Wallace's rhetoric were predominantly Baptist. They helped Wallace carry the Deep South and forced Nixon to mimic his message to carry the Outer South. The first Southern Baptist vote on elitism versus populism had been cast— and the populists won hands down. Why? Because in a climate of fear most people want a scrappy fighter to defend them, not a sophisticated technocrat to lecture them.

The most important consequence of this new mood for the South-ern Baptist Convention was that it reawakened an extreme conservatism, sometimes called fundamentalism, that had been gathering strength for years in a variety of churches—many of them Baptist. We know from the history of this movement in southern Christianity that it thrives on the kind of phobias that feed religious resentment. Asserting itself in the 1890s in response to fears of immigration, industrialization, and urban-ization that threatened a rurally-based Protestant hegemony, it reasserted itself in the 1920s in response to fears that Prohibition would be repealed, Darwinian evolution would undermine the Bible, and a Roman Catholic would be elected as U.S. president. Right on schedule it reappeared in the late 1960s in response to fears that legalizing abortion would cheapen the sanctity of life, that feminism would undermine the nuclear family, and that secularism would erode the spiritual foundations of the nation.

While the 1955-65 decade was a time of growth, confidence, and optimism in the SBC, the 1965-75 decade was a time of decline, conflict, and disappointment that saw great expectations go unfulfilled. The pincer-like effect of these countertrends created conditions in the 1975-85 decade that undermined moderate leadership in both politi-cal parties as well as in the denomination, opening the way for major changes to be pursued by the Religious Right.

During the 1955-65 decade, Southern Baptists adopted ambitious growth goals that committed them to numerical increase at a higher rate than in the past, such as the Thirty Thousand movement that would have doubled the number of churches and missions between 1956 and 1964. But by the 1965-75 decade, these goals were proving impossible to attain. Regarding numerical increase, the SBC continued to report more members each year, but these gains were not enough to keep pace with the growth of the general population. SBC membership as a percentage of southern whites of church-joining age peaked in 1960 and has declined ever since. For example, SBC membership rose from 9,732,000 in 1960 to 15,044,000 in 1990—which looks encouraging—but the percentage of Southern Baptists in the Deep South fell from 36 percent in 1960 to 31 percent in 1990. Regarding the rate of growth, SBC membership increased 34 percent during the 1950-59 decade but only 9.6 percent in the 1980-89 decade. Just as Southern Baptists began looking upward in an expansionist mood, all of the trend lines started turning downward.

Translated locally, this meant that many churches were finding it much more difficult to grow. Studies reported that as many as 80 percent of SBC churches were "plateaued," a euphemism for stagnation. What happened to congregations when the vice of attrition began to tighten?

Some churches tried to enlarge the prospect pool by lowering the acceptable age for membership, a few even dipping into the preschool years, but this strategy had obvious limits short of resorting to infant baptism. Others moved in the opposite direction as the median age of the congregation grew older, but this graying of the membership raised fears of "what will happen to our church when we are gone." Either way the money supply tightened because young children had no resources of their own and senior adults were moving into retirement on fixed incomes. Many churches that had erected new buildings and added staff in anticipation of rapid growth found themselves hard pressed to meet mortgage payments and payroll when these projections failed to materialize.

With this loss of momentum, church growth soon became the highest priority in congregational life, causing pastors to insist that the SBC furnish leadership in this area. After all, missions and evangelism had always been a dominant purpose of the denomination. Urgency was added to this agenda by the relentless numerical decline of mainline denominations such as Methodists, Presbyterians, and Episcopalians during the late sixties and seventies.[3] Unless the SBC did something different, it could share the same fate! In a search for solutions, Southern Baptists began to look outside their ranks for the first time, particularly at three groups that seemed to be successfully bucking the downward trend.

First, there were the non-establishment denominations, exclusivistic rather than ecumenical, that had stood aloof from the liberal trends of the fifties and early sixties such as the Assemblies of God, Seventh-Day Adventists, Nazarenes, Jehovah's Witnesses, and Mormons. These strict, authoritarian groups offered a simplistic, literalistic, absolutist faith of a kind that conservatives were seeking and, in contrast to their more effete upper-crust cousins, they were growing like kudzu![4]

Next, there were the independent or non-denominational descendants of fundamentalism, most of whom preferred to be called evangelicals. Setting out as an embattled minority in the fifties and early sixties, they soon challenged the religious status quo. With Billy Graham as their standard-bearer, Fuller Theological Seminary as their think-tank, and *Christianity Today* as their sounding board, this movement also zoomed in popularity during the late sixties and seventies even as the establishment denominations languished for lack of support.

Finally, the most market-conscious of all were the media preachers who spawned a new phenomenon called the Electronic Church. In the early days, most of these celebrities were dismissed as "religious entertainers" until the *Wall Street Journal* took a hard look at their balance sheets and reported a booming industry in which, as far back as 1977, the "take" of the top six superstars was in excess of $250 million and rapidly growing. Those familiar with religious finances immediately recognized that here were corporate empires bigger than whole denominations, all of them solidly ensconced on the ideological right.

Now for the key insight: Looking both at the decline of the mainline denominations positioned to the left and at the growth of free-wheeling religious movements positioned to the right, many Southern Baptists quite logically concluded that their future lay in following the strategy of the latter rather than the former. Add to this one other related factor: In those years, church growth experts were insisting that "homogeneous" groups grow much faster than heterogeneous groups simply because people like to be with their own kind.[5]

We have now isolated the two premises that those attempting a takeover of the SBC drew from their analysis of the American religious scene:

1. Success lay in positioning Southern Baptists as the only major denomination on the ideological right so as to reach a forgotten majority with whom the mainline denominations had lost contact in their drift to the left.
2. Such positioning would be effective only if all denominational agencies sent out a clear, consistent signal to the multitudes looking for a religion compatible with their ideological conservatism, and this could be done only by ridding the denomination of any employees not sympathetic with this orientation on the right.

These assumptions were not just theoretical deductions made by observing trends in other denominations, however. The takeover group insisted, with pardonable pride, that their hypotheses had already been tested on the most crucial anvil of all, the local congregation, notably by W. A. Criswell in the First Baptist Church of Dallas, Texas. With unflagging zeal, this intrepid pastor had staked out a position on the far right, refused to budge for four decades, invited those who differed with him to leave his flock, and in the process grown by far the largest church in the denomination! Criswell became the patriarch of the takeover group because what he did in Dallas provided a microcosm of the changes the group sought throughout the Convention. Nor was Criswell the only exemplar of this strategy, just the most prominent. Advocates of his approach could also point to dramatic growth in churches led by younger pastors such as Adrian Rogers at Bellevue Baptist Church in Memphis, Tennessee; Homer Lindsey, Jr., at the First Baptist Church in Jacksonville, Florida; and Charles Stanley at the First Baptist Church in Atlanta, Georgia, for confirmation that their strategy had produced the desired results.

All of the trends sketched to this point converged to impact negatively the morale of many Southern Baptist pastors. The sprawling bureaucracies of SBC agencies seemed increasingly remote to those in smaller churches, causing some of them to refer to the headquarters city of Nashville as "the SBC Vatican." Deeply invested in the lives of their members, they listened every day to fears and frustrations provoked by social disorder that the churches seemed helpless to prevent or to address. For a few minutes on Sunday morning they tried to talk sense to a troubled congregation, only to have their words lost in the inflammatory harangues of demagogic politicians and celebrity televangelists who dominated the mass media all week long. Their pulpit message might have had more clout if the church were growing, but the younger generation was dropping out of traditional churches in search of more innovative styles of worship.

Make no mistake: The 1965-75 decade was a tough time to be a successful pastor. You could sense it in shortened pastoral tenure as ministers moved from church to church searching in vain for a happy place to put down roots. Involuntary terminations steadily mounted, many of them exacerbated by racial turmoil not of the minister's making. The situation got so bad that the Baptist state papers began to editorialize on how to mediate internal disputes short of a public firing. Without bishops or judicatories to intervene in times of crisis, several state conventions established a full-time position in church-staff relations to deal with conflict resolution and placement problems. Lacking the protection of legal sanctions or even a mutually agreed-upon code of ethics to follow when resolving personnel issues, church employees began to feel vocationally vulnerable as attendance sagged and unrest spread.

How did the takeover group secure such enthusiastic support from their fellow pastors? The key to bolstering a stronger sense of authority was to make "inerrancy" the battle cry of the insurgency, a term they trumpeted to assert that every word of Scripture was "without error doctrinally, historically, scientifically, and philosophically." In other words, to preach the Bible correctly, which they insisted meant to preach it as "literally true," put one's message beyond challenge by grounding it in the eternal truth of God.

One problem with assigning unconditional authority to biblical preaching is that it tempts pastors to become authoritarian, thereby prompting a revolt of the laity. The inerrantists skillfully balanced the scales between pulpit and pew by insisting that grassroots Christians had the right to determine their own views of the Bible rather than depending on the findings of an intellectual elite with technical expertise. On the SBC Peace Committee (which worked from 1985-1988 to resolve conflict within the Convention), for example, Adrian Rogers was adamant that SBC seminaries should build their professional staffs and faculties from those who clearly reflected whatever dominant convictions and beliefs were held by Southern Baptists at large. In other words, the lay people rather than the scholarly professionals were to have the final say in what the denomination is to believe. He and Jerry Vines (who served two terms as SBC president, beginning in 1988) liked to stress the point in extreme fashion by insisting that if Southern Baptists believed pickles have souls, then the seminaries they support should teach just that!

Silly as it may sound, that oft-repeated slogan takes us to the heart of how inerrancy was actually being used in the SBC controversy. More than anything else, it was an effort to wrest control of what the Bible means from a handful of scholars with their endless technical problems and give it back to the churches where it would be preached passionately and believed on the basis of faith alone. The pastor would strongly influence the congregation by interpreting the Bible with authority, while the congregation would strongly influence the pastor by its response to that interpretation. Tenured scholars have lifetime job security needing only the approval of their peers, but pastors must continually reach people for their church or they will eventually be without a job. The inerrantists wanted the meaning of the Bible and the theology built upon it to emerge, not from a graduate seminar room, but from the dynamic interaction of pastor and people in a local congregation. Furthermore, they wanted the SBC seminaries to teach that understanding to their students.

To summarize: The times were out of joint. There was a sense of exhaustion with newer remedies of the moderates. Levels of destabilization and alienation were becoming toxic. Discontent had reached a tipping point where clinging to the status quo was viewed as a greater risk than going back to a simpler time. And so presuppositions were challenged, paradigms were shifted, and loyalties were renegotiated. Slowly but surely everything began to change, whether it be culture, politics, ideology, or religion. Some even thought that modernity itself, which had characterized Western civilization since the Enlightenment, was giving way to an as-yet-undefined postmodernity. It was simply impossible for a decentralized denomination as diverse and undisciplined as the SBC to escape being engulfed by this enormous ferment.

In the end, the militants won and the moderates lost because militancy rather than moderation was the mood of a majority of the messengers for many reasons, some of which have been summarized above. True to its democratic polity, which made no provision for protecting the rights of the minority, the SBC chose to pursue a course that resonated with the emerging mindset of its regional constituency. With a mixture of theological idealism and political realism, it decided to start what amounted to a new denomination—which is what it had done in 1845 when, caught in the toils of slavery and secession, the original SBC was established.

Notes

[1]The phrase is from Tom Shachtman, *Decade of Shocks: Dallas to Watergate, 1963-1974* (New York: Poseidon Press, 1983).

[2]The "Death of God" theology was reported most conspicuously in the cover story of *Time*, April 8, 1966, 82-87. Its leading interpreters were Thomas J. J. Altizer, William Hamilton, and Paul Van Buren.

[3]For an analysis of this trend, see Dean R. Hoge and David A. Roozen, eds., *Understanding Church Growth and Decline: 1950-1978* (New York: Pilgrim Press, 1979).

[4]The story was told from deep within the religious establishment by Dean M. Kelley, *Why Conservative Churches Are Growing* (New York: Harper & Row, 1972).

[5]Best known was C. Peter Wagner, *Our Kind of People* (Atlanta: John Knox Press, 1979).

CHAPTER 6

Applying Conservatism
and Liberalism: Partisan Politics

In both of the case studies just considered, the efforts of moderate
leaders to mediate between conservative and liberal positions met
with crushing defeats. In the biblical instance, all four of the leaders
had deep conservative roots in Judaism but were united around the liberal
conviction that Gentile converts were exempt from circumcision. In the
contemporary instance, agency heads with impeccable Baptist credentials
were supportive of seminaries that taught the latest in biblical criticism.

These disasters shared one characteristic in common that is seldom
emphasized but is crucial to our understanding of what actually
happened. I refer to the way that these moderate leaders were surprised,
even blindsided, by the outcome of their efforts. The solution offered by
the Jerusalem Conference was greeted with rejoicing (Acts 15:22, 31),
but almost immediately it began to collapse. The SBC agency heads were
confident that the pendulum would swing back to a centrist position;
instead, they were fired or forced to retire.

The overlooked dynamic contributing to these outcomes was partisan politics. Moderates like to emphasize the separation of church and
state, but this somehow translates as indifference to political developments. How to keep up in this area is not taught in seminaries, nor are
workshops offered at moderate meetings. Let us look more closely at this
dimension of our two case studies.

I

The New Testament period witnessed escalating tensions between
Judaism and its enemies. Palestine had been culturally conquered by the
Greeks and militarily conquered by the Romans. As a result, the Jewish
population felt threatened with assimilation into the foreign culture of
the Mediterranean world that would cause Judaism to disappear as a
distinctive way of life. The Jewish leadership of that day practiced the

politics of polarization, which eventually erupted in a fight to the finish against the mighty Roman Empire. Indeed, the apostolic era came to an abrupt end with the Jewish war of AD 66-73, which resulted in the fall of Jerusalem and the loss of a homeland in Palestine.

Since, in their ancient struggle for survival, the Jews had no flag around which to rally, they made circumcision the symbol of their embattled identity. Far from being an optional hygienic technique, circumcision became the boundary marker that separated Jews from the rest of the world (Eph. 2:11). Its decisive importance in first-century Judaism is seen clearly in Jubilees 15:26 from that era:

> And anyone who is born whose own flesh is not circumcised on the eighth day is not from the sons of the covenant which the Lord made for Abraham since (he is) from the children of destruction. And there is therefore no sign upon him so that he might belong to the Lord because (he is destined) to be destroyed and annihilated from the earth and to be uprooted from the earth because he has broken the covenant of the Lord our God.[1]

Aware of the sacred significance that the Jews were attaching to circumcision, their Greek and Roman masters pressured them to renounce what they viewed as a repugnant practice (1 Macc. 1:14-15). An operation to remove its mark surgically became common among the urban upper class and was viewed by the historian Josephus as forsaking Jewish customs to adopt a Greek way of life (*Jewish Antiquities*, XII, 241). Those who refused to repudiate circumcision were ostracized from the gymnasium, the public bath, and the athletic contests, all of which involved only males who participated in the nude. In some instances, the defiant practice of circumcision could lead to punitive taxation, loss of citizenship, or even death, as when the Seleucid overlord Antiochus IV Epiphanes slaughtered those families who circumcised their children and hung the infants from their mother's necks (1 Macc. 1:60-61, 2 Macc. 6:10). By the time Paul began his missionary work around 50 AD, circumcision had become the battle cry of patriotic Jews determined to avoid extinction as God's chosen people in a pagan culture.

Paul had been born and raised as an observant Jew, "circumcised on the eighth day" (Phil. 3:5). As we know from Romans 9-11, his heart's desire was to win his fellow countrymen (Rom. 10:1). Therefore, he was willing for Timothy to be circumcised to facilitate his acceptance by Jews in their synagogues (Acts 16:3), but he adamantly refused to require it of Titus, a Greek who would work primarily with Gentiles (Gal. 2:3). He knew that most non-Jews would never accept his message on condition of circumcision, because it would entangle them in a cultural and political controversy with which they wanted no part. This does not mean that Paul simply abandoned a practice clearly taught in his Hebrew Bible. Rather, he had learned from the martyr Stephen that the Abrahamic covenant of circumcision (Acts 7:8) failed to circumcise the heart and ears of the people, causing them to resist the Holy Spirit and reject God's messengers (Acts 7:51-53). Far from ignoring or repudiating circumcision, Paul internalized its meaning so that his Christianity would become a religion of the spirit rather than of the flesh (Col. 2:11-13).

Paul's insistence on eliminating circumcision from his gospel to the Gentiles was bound to result in open conflict with Jews (Gal. 2:4-5). Put as simply as possible, it raised the issue of what practices in Judaism one had to embrace in order to become a Christian. The first effort to address this problem resulted in what might be called a "two spheres" solution according to which there would be dual strategies: a mission to circumcised Jews led by Peter and a mission to uncircumcised Gentiles led by Paul (Gal. 2:7-9). Again and again, Paul tried to honor this compromise in evenhanded fashion (1 Cor. 7:18-19). After all, his driving passion was to win as many as possible regardless of whether they were Jew or Gentile (1 Cor. 9:19-22). For a brief time this strategy seemed to succeed as Christianity flourished, not only in Paul's Gentile churches, but also in the Jerusalem church led by James where "many thousands . . . among the Jews," who were "all zealous for the law," had become believers (Acts 21:20). The solution seemed so fair and simple: Gentiles did not have to become Jews in order to become Christians, nor did Jews have to become Gentiles in order to become Christians. It was to be a win/win solution for those on both sides of the issue.

Soon this strategy began to fail, precisely because of its success, as a growing number of Jewish Christians and Gentile Christians began to mingle in great cosmopolitan centers, such as Antioch. The reason for its failure was that a small but extreme group within the church called Judaizers refused to accept the "two spheres" accommodation but instead insisted that every Christian obey the ancestral customs of the Jews as set forth in the Hebrew Bible. These Judaizers organized themselves into "the circumcision party" and pressured Peter to stop eating with Gentile Christians in Antioch because they were not circumcised and did not observe kosher food requirements. In yielding to their pressure, Peter incurred the wrath of Paul who "opposed him to his face, because he stood condemned" (Gal. 2:11-12). By insisting on their understanding of the *purity* of the church, which involved a literalistic observance of such Old Testament practices as circumcision, the Judaizers were disrupting the *unity* of the church at the crucial point of table fellowship, which included the Lord's Supper.

As political and cultural tensions rapidly escalated in Palestine, the Judaizers increased their agitation by insisting that circumcision was essential to salvation (Acts 15:1). When this led to "no small dissension and debate" (Acts 15:2), it was decided to convene a summit in the Holy City, which we call the Jerusalem Conference. There a party of Pharisaic believers determined to prevail on the issue of circumcision by demanding that all Christians be "ordered to keep the law of Moses" (Acts 15:5). As mentioned earlier, both Peter and James sided with Barnabas and Paul, emphasizing that salvation was only "through the grace of the Lord Jesus," and therefore, Jewish requirements should not be imposed upon "Gentiles who were turning to God" (Acts 15:19).

With all of the key leaders in agreement, it might seem that the matter had finally been settled, but such was not the case. The next time that Paul returned to Jerusalem, he found a powder keg of political extremism ready to explode. This inflammatory attitude resulted in a riot based on a rumor that he might have carried a Gentile, Trophimus the Ephesian, into the Temple (Acts 21:27-32). Paul's life was spared by the intervention of Roman soldiers, but the rest of his ministry was spent as a prisoner processing judicial appeals to ever higher levels of the Roman government. No wonder he became so frustrated over the circumcision issue that, in exasperation, he invited those who were insisting on the circumcision of Gentiles apply the knife to themselves and be castrated (Gal. 5:12)! Paul washed his hands of the issue by insisting that circumcision simply did not matter to the Christian faith despite the claims of his detractors (Gal. 5:6, 6:15). To his heartbreak, the issue was finally settled, not by apostolic summitry, but by Roman armies that brutally crushed a suicidal uprising of Jews fomented by the kind of religious absolutism that had tried to wreck Paul's ministry.

II

Throughout most of the 1970s, conservative Southern Baptists were looking for new leadership to help them invent a new denomination. Most influential was an independent Baptist pastor in Lynchburg, Virginia named Jerry Falwell. His overarching imperative of "bringing America back to God" tapped into visceral fears of the laity who knew exactly what he was talking about. Moreover, he showed pastors how to become politically partisan in pressuring government to adopt their religious agenda, thereby thrusting them into a civic arena that had heretofore been the preserve of Roman Catholics and northern liberals. To say the least, things would never be the same again!

The formula for reclaiming America that Falwell mediated to his SBC friends required a close partnership between preachers willing to fight in the public square and politicians willing to implement the preachers' religious agenda in government. But where could a mutually beneficial alliance be forged? The Democratic Party was immediately rejected as being in the grip of northern liberals. The conservatism of Barry Goldwater and Richard Nixon was more appealing, but both of these Republican candidates were tone-deaf to the concerns of the Religious Right. George Wallace was an attractive alternative, his virulent racism notwithstanding, but, running as an independent, he could be only a political spoiler, and even that role was soon denied him by a would-be assassin's bullet. And so the religious revolutionaries bided their time through the late sixties and early seventies, building their counter-cultural churches and waiting for an opportune moment to strike.

Timing is of the essence in executing a successful strategy, and in the late 1970s two developments coincided that played perfectly into the hands of the Religious Right in general and the SBC insurgents in particular. The first was the emergence of Ronald Reagan on the national scene in his strong but unsuccessful bid to wrest the Republican nomination from sitting President Gerald Ford in 1976. Once Ford lost that election to Jimmy Carter, Reagan quickly became both a frontrunner for the 1980 Republican nomination and a favorite of conservative preachers looking for a political ally. Once Reagan secured his party's nomination, a national affairs briefing was held on August 21-22, 1980, in Dallas that was intended, according to Conservative Caucus leader Ed McAteer, "not to endorse a political party or candidate, but to pledge allegiance to principles." Reagan responded by remarking, "I know you can't endorse me because this is a non-partisan meeting . . . but I endorse you." Now the SBC takeover leaders had on their side a soon-to-be president of the United States!

Just as Reagan was adding the Religious Right to his political coalition, the South was becoming a competitive two-party region for the first time since the Civil War.[2] As late as 1964, there was not a single Republican senator from the South, Strom Thurmond of South Carolina becoming the first by changing parties. Only two Republican representatives out of 105 were in the southern House delegation. Ironically, it was a southern President Lyndon Johnson who contributed most to the breakup of the Democratic "Solid South" by signing the Civil Rights Act of 1964 and the Voting Rights Act of 1965, by the liberal social-spending policies of his Great Society programs, and by his inability to win the Vietnam War. Nixon exploited growing Democratic discontent with his "Southern Strategy" in the landslide election of 1972,[3] but it was Reagan who enabled Republicans to displace Democrats as the plurality party among southern white voters.

This historic shift played itself out predictably in SBC life beginning with the 1980 presidential campaign.[4] The challenger was a nominal non-resident member of a Disciples of Christ church whose religious participation was minimal at best, who had long struggled with family problems, and who gravitated toward a neo-apocalyptic theology that was peripheral to Christian orthodoxy. The incumbent, by contrast, was a quintessential Southern Baptist moderate who actively taught Sunday School as a serious Bible student, who went on mission trips building houses for the poor, and who faithfully attended church even in Washington during his presidency.

Then why did the Religious Right in general, and Southern Baptists in particular, reject Carter so decisively almost as soon as he took office? Because he accommodated the more liberal wing of his party led by the formidable Edward M. Kennedy while Reagan purged his party of moderate "Rockefeller Republicans." Because he sought to downplay the Communist threat whereas Reagan later exacerbated it by describing the Soviet Union as an "evil empire." Because he sought input from those with alternative understandings of the family while Reagan championed the traditional view of family values.

By an amazing stroke of good fortune for SBC insurgents, the 1980 presidential election became a referendum on moderate versus militant leadership, Carter and Reagan being ideal to play those roles, and the moderate option was solidly trounced. The denominational militants could not have timed their takeover strategy better to coincide with the moment of greatest political opportunity.

Once the needed partnership with Reagan was sealed by his victory, the increasing dominance of militants in the SBC paralleled almost exactly the growing strength of the Republican Party among southern white voters. For example, in 1988, when the SBC controversy had almost been won by the militants, the elder George Bush tallied more votes in every southern state than Reagan received in 1980 even though Bush had been identified earlier with the moderate wing of the Republican party. In 2004, when the denominational takeover was complete, the younger George Bush—as quintessential a militant as Carter was a moderate—swept the South so completely that he carried more than 90 percent of the counties where whites were a majority of the population.

III

Partisan politics is powerful in settling controversy for at least two reasons. First, the mass media always insure that political contention will saturate the American mind especially as an election campaign nears its climax. For more than a year the presidential candidates are overexposed through endless stump speeches, talk shows, interviews, and formal debates. Billions of dollars are spent to bombard voters with seductive advertising designed to secure their commitment to a particular ticket. By contrast, the SBC presidency is decided early in a two-day annual gathering based on a brief nominating speech backed by word-of-mouth campaigning without benefit of budget. It is true that what appears to be an informal process producing a spontaneous result can be manipulated behind the scenes to build support for a candidate among those in attendance, but the great majority of SBC members will have never seen or heard the winner or have any idea what issues were at stake in the outcome. This is only to say that partisan politics is vastly more influential than doctrinal disputes in shaping the Southern Baptist mindset.

The second reason why the secular political process proved so influential is that it was not very secular. Candidates for public office do not talk about how they would actually govern if elected. Rather, they try to present a compelling case for how they would fulfill the nation's mission, achieve its highest vision, and be true to its core values. Which is exactly the agenda on which the Religious Right agreed with Reagan Republicans in forming their partnership. As a result, beginning in the 1980 presidential campaign, the religious message of the former began to coalesce with the political message of the latter. To put it rhetorically, conservative politicians and preachers learned to talk alike. This gave the SBC takeover group a huge advantage because they were able to ride the coattails—free of charge!—of the most powerful decision-making process in American culture.

Politics has been called a barometer of the *Zeitgeist*; that is, it constantly takes the pulse of the national mood. By 1979, a frustrated America was ready to consider moving in a completely new direction. The SBC, as "the Established Church of Dixie"—a religious expression of "the southern way of life"—could not avoid facing the same choice. If Jimmy Carter had convinced southern white voters that his moderate approach to presidential leadership was in their best interests, the denominational decision might have been different—but he was not able to do so. (In my first pastorate during the early 1950s, I did not have a single church member who was openly Republican. Everyone was still a Yellow Dog Democrat. In my last pastorate during the late 1970s, I did not have a single church member who was an open supporter of Carter.)

IV

Now that we have looked in more detail at the political background of our case studies, it is possible to state some principles that are often relevant to religious controversy.

1. *Conservatism is motivated by fear and liberalism by hope.* The great fear of conservatives is anarchy, change so rapid and radical that it threatens to sweep away the hard-earned gains of the past. The great hope of liberals is for progress by appealing to the conscience and creativity of humanity to develop those forces that contribute to freedom.

In the first century it was easy for Palestinian Jews to be fearful, and therefore conservative, because Rome was actively pursuing a program of Hellenization to corrupt their distinctive culture that was the source of their solidarity as a people. By contrast, the leaders of the early church were hopeful, and therefore liberal on circumcision, because of the success of their Gentile mission.

In the twentieth century, it was easy for white southerners to be fearful of federal legislation pouring out of Washington that would change their traditional culture. To fear add frustration over their failure to find a safe haven from the big government blitz in Reagan Republicanism. The South's refusal to join the rest of the nation—indeed to spite it—stood in sharp contrast to its better universities. There, where new perspectives and discoveries are prized more than old traditions, the liberal quest reigns supreme on the humanities faculty and among many of its graduates. Indeed, many students aspire to work in an academic culture despite its expensive preparation, lengthy apprenticeship, and modest wages. They join a crowded applicant pool to compete for scarce positions because they want to use their newfound knowledge to enrich the society to which their students return.[5]

2. *Culture is the catalyst and politics the driver of public attention.* In colonial times the "parson" was a primary source of information and issues who shaped the viewpoint of his hearers and their village. Today, preachers are hopelessly outclassed by politicians in the use of mass media to sway public attitudes because of the vast resources at their disposal. The only competition is mounted by the marketers who incessantly bombard us with saturation advertising. Both make extensive use of television, radio, newspapers, computers, tapes, magazines, books, and pamphlets. The new frontier is to make every media device mobile so that its message will not only go global, but also will reach the most remote spots on Planet Earth. The media have long been accused of a liberal bias, particularly newspapers in their editorial policy, doubtless caused by the history of crusading so cherished by journalists.

3. *Very few people possess the sophistication to adopt one ideology politically and another religiously.* Ideological labels tend to become identity markers in most areas of life. When one says "I am a conservative" or "I am a liberal," that assumption is likely to cover a person's views on politics, economics, and religion. To be sure, there are multitudes of books limited to each of these subjects. So carefully drawn are specializations on college campuses that very few political scientists would feel competent to comment on religion. Even more important, churchgoers drawn from many careers do not live in the book culture. They have never even heard of most of the books cited in this study.

4. *We honor the dominant ideology of those with whom we work.* Let me use my home state of Alabama to illustrate. The Gallup Daily tracking

identified Alabama as the most conservative state in the nation for 2012 by the self-designation of those polled. Here are the averages in the ideological categories offered by Gallup:[6]

Ideology	Alabama	United States
Conservative	51%	38%
Moderate	32%	36%
Liberal	15%	23%

There is one important limitation to this information: its failure to distinguish between black and white respondents. Blacks identify themselves as liberals much more than whites do because they depend on an aggressive central government to address their exploitation by the white power structure. Again, Gallup found only a 69 percent correlation nationally between conservatism and support of the Republican Party. All over the South are blacks who prefer to style themselves as conservatives based on business success, but who would not think of abandoning the Democratic Party.

In the South we still have a two-party culture, but the two parties work in the same way. Back out the black data and we are left with white southern churches with a high percentage of conservative Republicans in their membership. Compare election results with denominational loyalties, such as SBC support, and you will see a close correlation between supporting a conservative political party and a conservative church denomination.

5. *There is strength in allegiance to only one ideology.* It takes a thoughtful and inquisitive person to harvest ideas from culturally competitive positions, which is why mediating movements are usually marginal rather than mainstream. Moderates seldom become religious leaders of large organizations unless they successfully align with conservatives or liberals. The predominantly white Baptist movement in the South is served by the conservative Southern Baptist Convention (SBC), the moderate Cooperative Baptist Fellowship (CBF), and the liberal Alliance of Baptists (AOB). Their size is as follows:

Denomination	Churches	Members
SBC	45,764	15,978,112
CBF	1,800	750,000
AOB	140	3,300

Seminaries represent a special case. Like universities offering graduate education, faculties are more liberal than the sponsoring churches. This tension is exacerbated when the faculty uses the latest complex methodologies to come up with something novel that could not possibly be understood by almost half of the SBC pastors who lack even a basic seminary degree. As early as 1968, it was not difficult to discern that the SBC was rapidly becoming monolithically conservative and Republican. Holdouts were the historically important tall-steeple churches whose pastors often had doctoral degrees. Seminary faculty members were welcome in such churches, but they were few in number and waning in influence.

6. *Despite their minority status, moderates can have a disproportionate influence by forging ties with one of the major traditions.* After all, they deliberately seek to learn from both traditions, whereas conservatives and liberals, lacking the corrective stimulus of the other side, become inbred and overcommitted to views hammered out in another era and eventually suffer from cultural exhaustion. American life alternates between several cycles, giving moderates abundant opportunities to work in the transition.[7]

7. *In coping with the intensity of polarized controversy, we do not succumb to the Manichean heresy.* In the third century AD lived a prophet named Mani. With a dualistic Zoroastrian background, he taught that all reality is locked in a cosmic struggle between good and evil. As a settled attitude, one looks for an adversary and this very presupposition tends to highlight differences rather than similarities.[8]

V

With religious and political principles before us drawn from biblical and contemporary sources, we are ready to apply these insights to the greatest controversy ever to engulf Baptists in the South. I shall draw on my own experience simply because I know it best. In my recent writings I have advocated that moderates form ties with conservatives.[9] Because this suggestion was greeted with courteous contempt ranging from "unworkable" to "impossible," I have selected illustrations that fall into that category:

Baptists magnify the *local* congregational unit above all others, so I begin there. I was pastor of the First Baptist Church in Shreveport, Louisiana for twelve years (1975-1987) that coincided with the heart of the SBC controversy. Shreveport is often called "the buckle on the

Bible Belt," and its flagship church lived up to that billing: segregated, male-dominated, living on the memory of a golden age under M. E. Dodd (1912-1950). The congregation badly needed a dose of liberalism, and I used the pulpit to administer it. Looking back on my preaching there after leaving Shreveport, I wrote an entire book on how to restore the liberal dimension of Christian proclamation without ever using that word.

After the church balanced its living out of the future with its living out of the past, it was difficult but rewarding to maintain that balance in a predominantly conservative culture I could hardly change. About a dozen families left when we racially integrated the membership and less than a dozen when we began ordaining women to the diaconate and ministry, but more than that number joined us because they applauded rather than opposed these practices.

Doubtless we were viewed in Baptist circles as a "liberal" church for a time because we were the first congregation in our parish (county) and state to make such changes. In retrospect, however, such innovations seemed modest indeed, particularly when compared to the rate of change in other areas of public life.

Pastors persuaded that the people of God should conserve everything of Christ that has already been implemented and liberate everything of Christ that has not yet been implemented will succeed as religious leaders in the Deep South if they learn to affirm conservatives, moderates, and liberals equally. To the naysayers convinced that this is simply impossible, I would say: Look to the churches where it goes on all the time!

Those who realize this but want a fallback position will argue that the training of preachers must conform to the views of those in charge of its support, organizationally what we know as the *state* level. When I came to Samford University as its provost, the campus was surrounded by strong moderate churches that were greatly outnumbered by a host of conservative churches throughout Alabama. In my first year (1987-88), a Presbyterian layman gave Samford a gift adequate to establish the first fully accredited seminary in Alabama. To the strategic post of founding dean I appointed Timothy George, clearly the finest scholar in the conservative movement. Soon thereafter, an entire generation of faculty began to retire from the religion department. Needing new leadership, I appointed as chair of the department Bill Leonard, the most influential speaker and premier historian of the moderate movement.

Despite the impeccable credentials of both men, despite the theological balance that they brought to our campus life, despite their distinguished speaking and writing assignments that spread the Samford name where it had never gone before, I took a lot of grief over both appointments from the "impossible" crowd. Moderates were quick to assert that I had fatally compromised the new divinity school, while conservatives wanted to fire me for playing partisan politics. Both sides assured me that they could *never* support the leader on whom they had heaped such contempt.

Unfortunately for my bitter critics, their doom-and-gloom scenarios failed to materialize. Both the divinity school and the religion department flourished with new leadership. Timothy George's early faculty additions were quintessential moderates (Fisher Humphreys and William O'Brien). George and Leonard debated such prickly subjects as Calvinism in campus-wide forums, modeling their personal friendship as well as the academic courtesies so sorely lacking in their detractors.

I came away from this whole episode convinced that it is not healthy for either conservatives or moderates to associate only with their own ideological crowd. It makes them too totalitarian in what they claim, too contemptuous of those who differ with them, and too dependent on group loyalty to risk diversity.

Although the SBC controversy spread to many churches and schools, it was focused on the twenty *national* agencies funded by the Convention, particularly the six seminaries. The climax came with the appointment of the "Peace Committee" on which I served to investigate the causes of and recommend solutions to the SBC controversy.

In the midst of our discussions, questions often arose regarding the meaning of inerrancy. Differences surfaced over what the term means to scholars and what it means to SBC inerrantists unfamiliar with their work. To clarify and contend for the latter, Adrian Rogers hastily jotted down four popular convictions held about Scripture. By the time of our final report, this spontaneous illustration had become what the committee had "found" throughout the SBC:

- They believe in direct creation of mankind, and therefore they believe Adam and Eve were real persons.
- They believe that the named authors did indeed write the biblical books attributed to them by those books.

- They believe that the miracles described in Scripture did indeed occur as supernatural events in history.
- They believe that the historical narratives given by biblical authors are indeed accurate and reliable as given by those authors.

At first I was scandalized by this list, skillfully selected to repudiate the work of scholars—even that of scholarly inerrantists. It seemed indifferent to the things "most" Southern Baptists believed based on Scripture that have long since been repudiated, such as slavery. By challenging the legitimacy and importance of biblical scholarship, it tested whether I could work with conservative leaders such as these. During the almost forty years since then, my mind has gradually changed regarding the issues involved. To explain my transition, permit me to summarize a page from our family history.

My father was one of eight children born on a subsistence farm in Coosa County, Alabama. So poor were their circumstances that most of the men migrated to nearby cities in search of work. But two of the brothers, Walter and Carey, stayed behind to look after their aging mother and their two unmarried sisters. Suffice it to say that they were pillars of the Providence Baptist Church, the only hub in a community that had no crossroad, post office, or general store. Regardless of the weather, they were always at church even if it meant hitching up their two mules—Joe and Nellie—to the wagon as the only means of transportation for the women.

Now for the breakthrough insight: Both Walter and Carey doubtless believed all four points for which Adrian Rogers contended. Why? Because they had only one Bible (KJV), thus nothing to compare it to since 1611. Because their pastor for thirty-nine years, the beloved Brother J. D. Hughes received only a high school education in nearby Rockford. Because the brothers received only an elementary education, hardly adequate to understand the findings of seminary faculty based on at least sixteen additional years of schooling.

Despite my sharp contentions with Rogers, I eventually decided not to argue with my uncles on these contested points. Why? Because what they lacked in scholarship, they more than made up for in piety. They loved the Bible, read the Bible, and believed the Bible in ways that would put some seminarians to shame.

This did not mean that I capitulated to the brandishments of Rogers. Rather, it meant a fresh realization on my part that scholarly findings should be shared with those prepared to understand and appreciate at least minimally how the results were reached. I have benefitted greatly from scholarly approaches to Scripture and gladly shared the fruits of those labors with the Providence Baptist Church. Moreover, I remonstrated with Rogers before his untimely death not to fight what he had never tried. I am not going to spend my final time on earth fighting the Walters and Careys in the SBC. Anyone who wants to know and live by Scripture is a friend of mine.

Having chosen illustrations from local, state, and national levels, I conclude this section with a look at *international* Baptist life. From 1970-90, I held a variety of leadership positions in the study and research division of the Baptist World Alliance. My most sensitive assignment was to plan programs that honored the enormous diversity of our member bodies and yet invite speakers who could treat the assigned topic in ways that would bring us together.

Take the Russians and the Germans. For years, Baptist life in the Soviet Union had been badly split making it unpredictable who might receive a visa to attend the annual BWA leadership meeting. One year, when the Russian delegation was large enough for one person to attend our Commission on Baptist Doctrine, we were eager to hear from him although he had to speak through a translator and had not attended one day of seminary (all theological schools in his area had been closed by the government).

Also scheduled to speak was a regular member of the Commission, a German fluent in English who had studied with the theological faculty of a great university in his homeland. As such, he could work in Hebrew, Greek, and Latin sources and employ the complex historical-critical methodology for which the Germans are famous. He was not at all a show-off with his scholarship; it was simply the way he had been trained.

Once again the classic issue: The Russian was what we would call a fundamentalist, and the German was a biblical critic. The former was likely to accept and the latter to reject most of Adrian Rogers' four tests. So what did we do in our meeting? At my urging, both men described their training: mentoring in the home of a veteran pastor versus formal lectures in a crowded classroom. The two presenters communicated briefly on the strengths and weaknesses of their training, and then I opened the floor for a vigorous discussion on which both approaches took their bumps. No one was belittled and, as the saying goes, "a good time was had by all."

In light of my experience at every level of Baptist life, I do have to wonder where all of this talk about "impossible" comes from. To be sure it is difficult, but should the reconciliation between Christians be more difficult than the reconciliation of unbelievers to God? How can we talk about loving one another and then show disdain for those who understand some debated point of doctrine differently? Are we willing to pray for a Spirit-inspired change of heart, daring to reach across chasms of contempt and affirm—indeed embrace—those of every ideology, all of which were nailed to the cross when God through Christ reconciled the world unto himself (2 Cor. 5:17, Eph. 2:15)?

Notes

[1] James H. Charlesworth, ed., *The Old Testament Pseudepigrapha*, 2 (Garden City, NY: Doubleday, 1985), 87.

[2] On this shift, see the many works of Earl Black and Merle Black, esp. *The Rise of Southern Republicans* (Cambridge: Belknap Press, 2002).

[3] On the development of this "Southern Strategy," see the work of Baptist deacon and lay minister Harry S. Dent, *The Prodigal South Returns to Power* (New York: John Wiley & Sons, 1978).

[4] For a detailed study, see Oran P. Smith, *The Rise of Baptist Republicanism* (New York: New York University Press, 1997).

[5] Neil Gross, *Why Are Professors Liberal and Why Do Conservatives Care?* (Cambridge: Harvard University Press, 2013).

[6] Frank Newport, *Alabama, North Dakota, Wyoming Most Conservative States*, Gallup, February 1, 2013, http://www.gallup.com/poll/160196/alabama-north-dakota-wyoming-conservative-states.aspx.

[7] Arthur Schlesinger Jr., *The Cycles of American History* (Boston: Houghton Miflin, 1986).

[8] For a comprehensive approach to history avoiding Manichean perspective, see David Cannadine, *The Undivided Past: Humanity Beyond Our Differences* (New York: Alfred A. Knopf, 2013).

[9] William E. Hull, *Strategic Preaching: The Role of the Pulpit in Pastoral Leadership* (St. Louis: Chalice Press, 2006).

CONCLUSION

The first thing we learn from these ideological struggles is that Christianity is not an otherworldly escapist religion but one that addresses persons in their own distinctive setting and seeks to become indigenous in that culture. Because of its rootedness in the real world of time and place, earthly pressures on the faith can become enormous. Particularly potent is the combination of patriotism and piety that seeks to make the church an agent of some group's political agenda. Religious people take seriously their earthly citizenship as well as their ethnic identity, and they desire to be loyal to their inherited traditions.

In Jewish Christianity this led to the emergence of a "circumcision party," whereas in our country it has resulted in a strong tradition of exclusivism with its frequently violent expressions of hostility to anything foreign. Sad to say, religion has often been in the forefront of strident efforts to sanctify sameness and demonize differences. A "churchly" component was included even in the Klu Klux Klan with its Bible-thumping tirades against Catholics, Jews, and Blacks in its ritualistic use of white robes of purity and in its obscene use of fiery crosses as symbols of terror.

Second, in light of our enormous cultural diversity, it is not only legitimate but also often necessary to have multiple strategies for evangelization. In the New Testament, this required one approach to Jews and another to Gentiles. Today it may require different approaches to the first world and the third world, to the older generation and the younger generation, and to liberals and conservatives. The remarkable thing is that, no matter how diverse our culture becomes, the spirit of Christ has a universal appeal to all groups regardless of their nationality, gender, political persuasion, or ideological preference.

Third, when we seek to resolve the tension between the particularity of our religious customs and the universality of our risen Lord, doctrinaire extremists can wreak havoc and subvert the worldwide outreach of the Christian faith regardless of the solutions we devise. Everyone in the early church saw the split coming as Paul made his final appeal in the Holy City (Acts 21:1-12); yet, they seemed powerless to halt the momentum of his enemies' reckless hysteria until it had wrought division and destruction on every hand.

Fourth, even when an impasse is reached, that does not mean we throw up our hands in despair. Rather, as Paul reassured the apprehensive

Christians of Caesarea, our only choice is not between the two sides in whatever culture war may be raging. We need not be stymied if various Christian groups reach a point where they cannot reconcile their differences. Our faith stands or falls, not on our ability to solve all of the problems presented by our diverse backgrounds, but on the credibility of Christ himself to redeem those of every background. Only God is the providential Lord of history who can use even our disagreements to accomplish his will (Acts 21:14).

Fifth, it was the struggle over circumcision that brought Christianity to the Gentiles. If the Judaizers had won, if customs such as circumcision had been made mandatory for salvation, then Christianity would have become little more than a small reforming sect within Judaism. Why is it that we may readily embrace the Christian faith even if we have no Jewish background? It is because Paul fought to the death for our right to do so.

Sixth, our churches are engaged in a global mission stretching around the world. Why should we invest so much time and effort and money to help those in such different cultures? What do we as Americans have to offer Asians or Latinos? Why not just stay home and help our own kind? Because we have something utterly crucial to offer every person in the world if we will but do so, not as Americans, but as Christians. Ours is not a national or ethnic faith like Judaism. Rather, we discover what is essential when we go outside our culture to win those who do not share our inherited practices.

Seventh, when faced with conflict, we would do well to follow these principles: Do not commit your faith to one side in the latest culture wars but to the spirit of Christ who is Lord of all cultures. Go with those who are trying to reach all peoples across every barrier. Avoid the polarizers who often win in the short term, but embrace the reconcilers who are often vindicated by the longer march of history. Mutual cooperation between conservatives and liberals is what opened Christianity to all the peoples of the world.

BIBLIOGRAPHY

Conservatism

Auerbach, Morton. *The Conservative Illusion.* New York: Columbia University Press, 1959.

Buckley, William F. Jr., ed. *Did You Ever See a Dream Walking? American Conservative Thought in the Twentieth Century.* Indianapolis: Bobbs-Merrill, 1970.

Guttman, Allen. *The Conservative Tradition in America.* New York: Oxford University Press, 1967.

Kirk, Peter. *The Conservative Mind: From Burke to Eliot,* 3rd ed. Chicago: Regnery Publishing, 1960.

Kirk, Russell, ed. *The Portable Conservative Reader.* New York: Viking Press, 1982.

Lora, Ronald. *Conservative Minds in America.* New York: Rand McNally, 1971.

Nash, George H. *The Conservative Intellectual Movement in America: Since 1945.* New York: Basic Books, 1976.

Rossiter, Clinton. *Conservatism in America: The Thankless Persuasion,* 2nd ed. New York: Vintage Books, 1962.

Viereck, Peter R. *Conservatism Revisited,* rev. ed. New York: Free Press, 1966.

Witonski, Peter, ed. *The Wisdom of Conservatism.* New Rochelle, NY: Arlington House, 1971.

Liberalism

Bramsted, S. K. and K. J. Melhuish, eds. *Western Liberalism: A History in Documents from Locke to Croce.* London: Longmans, 1978.

Bullock, Alan and Maurice Shock, eds. *Liberal Tradition: From Fox to Keynes.* New York: Oxford University Press, 1967.

Freeden, Michael. *The New Liberalism: An Ideology of Social Reform.* New York: Oxford University Press, 1978.

Girvetz, Harry K. *The Evolution of Liberalism,* rev. ed. New York: Collier Books, 1963.

Hartz, Louis. *The Liberal Tradition in America.* New York: Harcourt, Brace, 1955.

Mansfield, Harvey C. Jr. *The Spirit of Liberalism.* Cambridge: Harvard
    University Press, 1978.
Minogue, Kenneth R. *The Liberal Mind.* New York: Random House,
    1963.
Orton, W. A. *The Liberal Tradition.* New Haven: Yale University Press,
    1945.
Schapiro, Jacob S. *Liberalism: Its Meaning and History.* Princeton: Van
    Nostrand, 1958.
Strauss, Leo. *Liberalism, Ancient and Modern.* New York: Basic Books,
    1968.
Trilling, Lionel. *The Liberal Imagination.* Garden City, NY: Doubleday,
    1950.

ABOUT THE AUTHOR

WILLIAM EDWARD HULL, research professor at Samford University in Birmingham, Alabama, died on December 10, 2013, after a five-year struggle with ALS. During the years of his sickness, he produced six books that were published under the ad-hoc Hull Legacy Series committee of Mountain Brook Baptist Church in Birmingham. An additional manuscript was published posthumously. Mountain Brook Baptist Church collected and digitized the sermons and lectures he produced as theologian in residence. He was the subject of many articles and was honored in the journal *Perspectives in Religious Studies*, summer 2010.

PERSONAL

Birth:
> May 28, 1930, Birmingham, Alabama

Parents:
> William E. Hull (1888-1974)
> Margaret J. King Hull (1887-1974)

Wife:
> Wylodine Hester Hull (1931-2012)
> Married July 26, 1952

Children:
> David William, born August 21, 1955
> Susan Virginia, born November 6, 1957

EDUCATION

Public School:
> Birmingham, Alabama School System, 1936-48
> Graduate, Phillips High School, January 1948

College:
> University of Alabama, 1948-50 (pre-medical studies)
> Samford University, Birmingham, Alabama, 1950-51 (B.A. in religion, May 1951)

Graduate School:
> The Southern Baptist Theological Seminary (M.Div., May 1954;
> Ph.D., New Testament major, January 1960)

Advanced Study:
> University of Göttingen, Germany, 1962-63
> Harvard University, 1971

ACADEMIC

New Testament Department, The Southern Baptist Theological Seminary:
> Fellow, 1954-55
> Instructor, 1955-58
> Assistant Professor, 1958-61
> Associate Professor, 1961-67
> Professor, 1967-75

Baptist Theological Seminary, Rüschlikon, Switzerland:
    Visiting Professor, 1963
Louisiana State University School of Medicine:
    Visiting Professor, 1975-78
The Southern Baptist Theological Seminary:
    Visiting Professor, 1979, 1990-92
Nigerian Baptist Theological Seminary:
    Visiting Professor, 1982
Samford University:
    University Professor, 1987-2000
    Research Professor, 2000-2013

ADMINISTRATIVE

The Southern Baptist Theological Seminary:
    Chairman, New Testament Department, 1958-60, 1963-68
    Director of Graduate Studies, School of Theology, 1968-70
    Dean, School of Theology, 1969-75
    Provost, 1972-75
Samford University:
    Provost, 1987-96
    Acting President, 1993

MINISTERIAL

Ordained:
    Dawson Memorial Baptist Church, Birmingham, Alabama, 1950
Pastor:
    Beulah Baptist Church, Wetumpka, Alabama, 1950-51
    Cedar Hill Baptist Church, Owenton, Kentucky, 1952-53
    First Baptist Church, New Castle, Kentucky, 1953-58
    First Baptist Church, Shreveport, Louisiana, 1975-87
Theologian in Residence:
    Mountain Brook Baptist Church, Birmingham, Alabama, 1991-2013
Interim Minister:
    Highland Baptist Church, Louisville, Kentucky, 1966-67
    Metropolitan Baptist Church, Cambridge, Massachusetts, 1971
    Crescent Hill Baptist Church, Louisville, Kentucky, 1972
    Vestavia Hills Baptist Church, Birmingham, Alabama, 1988-89
    Riverchase Baptist Church, Birmingham, Alabama, 1989
    Southside Baptist Church, Birmingham, Alabama, 1990-91
    Huffman Baptist Church, Birmingham, Alabama, 1996-97
Speaker:
    "The Baptist Hour"
    Baptist World Alliance
    Southern Baptist Convention
    Cooperative Baptist Fellowship General Assembly
    Southern Baptist Pastors' Conference
    Ridgecrest and Glorieta Baptist Conference Centers

Baptist State Conventions
Evangelistic Conferences and Assemblies
Baptist Missions in Europe, Middle East, Southeast Asia
U.S. Air Force Preaching Missions in Turkey

DENOMINATIONAL

Northwest Louisiana Baptist Association:
    Executive Board, 1975-87
    Long Range Planning Committee, 1976-78
    Chairman, Public Affairs Committee, 1979-81
Louisiana Baptist Convention:
    Louisiana College: Trustee, 1978-85, 1986-87 (Chairman, 1980-82);
    Board of Development, 1985-87
    Committee on Order of Business, 1976-79 (Chairman, 1978-79)
    Convention Sermon, 1980
    Resolutions Committee, 1983-86
Southern Baptist Convention:
    President, National Association of Baptist Professors of Religion, 1967-68
    Representative to North American Baptist Fellowship, 1980-85
    Convention Sermon, 1982
    Peace Committee, 1985-88
Baptist World Alliance:
    Commission on Baptist Doctrine, 1970-75 (Chairman, 1970-75)
    Commission on Doctrine and Interchurch Cooperation, 1975-80
    Commission on Pastoral Leadership, 1980-90 (Chairman, 1980-85)
    Division Committee on Study and Research, 1980-90 (Chairman, 1980-85)

ORGANIZATIONAL

American Academy of Political and Social Science
American Academy of Religion
American Association for Higher Education
American Association of University Professors
American Schools of Oriental Research
Society of Biblical Literature

LECTURESHIPS

Theological Fellowship:
    Southwestern Baptist Theological Seminary, 1965
Throgmorton Lectures:
    Southern Illinois University, 1972
Staley Distinguished Christian Scholar Lectures:
    Mobile College, 1973
    Baptist College at Charleston, 1978
    Samford University, 1978, 1982
    Louisiana College, 1986

Harwell Lectures:
    Auburn University, 1973
    University of Alabama, 1973
Spell Lectures:
    Mississippi College, 1977
Deere Lectures:
    Golden Gate Baptist Theological Seminary, 1983
Hester Lectures:
    Association of Southern Baptist Colleges and Schools, 1996
Nelson Lectures:
    Samford University, 2002
Self Preaching Lectures:
    McAfee School of Theology, 2004
Holley-Hull Lectures:
    Samford University, 2004
Harry Vaughan Smith Lectures:
    Mercer University, 2005

PUBLICATIONS (BOOKS)

Dissertation:
    The Background of the New Temple Concept in Early Christianity
    (Ph.D., The Southern Baptist Theological Seminary, 1959).
Author:
    The Gospel of John, "Alpha-Omega Series" (Broadman Press, 1964)
    "John," *Broadman Bible Commentary*, vol. 9, pp. 189-376 (Broadman Press, 1970)
    The Bible: How To Study It (Covenant Press, 1974)
    Beyond the Barriers (Broadman Press, 1981)
    Love in Four Dimensions (Broadman Press, 1982)
    The Christian Experience of Salvation, "Layman's Library of Christian Doctrine,"
        vol. 9 (Broadman Press, 1987)
    Southern Baptist Higher Education: Retrospect and Prospect (Samford University
        Press, 2001)
    The Quest for Spiritual Maturity (Samford University Press, 2004)
    The Four-Way Test: Core Values of the Rotary Movement (Rotary Club of
        Birmingham, 2004)
    Strategic Preaching: The Role of the Pulpit in Pastoral Leadership (Chalice Press,
        2006)
    The Meaning of the Baptist Experience (Baptist History and Heritage Society, 2007)
    Harbingers of Hope: Claiming God's Promises in Today's World (Samford University
        Press, 2007)
    The Quest for a Good Death: A Christian Guide (Samford University Press, 2014)
Contributor:
    Professor in the Pulpit (Broadman Press, 1963)
    The Truth That Makes Men Free (Broadman Press, 1966)
    Salvation in Our Time (Broadman Press, 1978)
    Set Apart for Service (Broadman Press, 1980)
    Celebrating Christ's Presence Through the Spirit (Broadman Press, 1981)
    The Twentieth Century Pulpit, Volume II (Abingdon, 1981)

Ministers Manual (Doran's) (Harper & Row, 1983-1987)
Biblical Preaching: An Expositor's Treasury (Westminster Press, 1983)
Preaching in Today's World (Broadman Press, 1984)
Heralds to a New Age (Brethren Press, 1985)
Getting Ready for Sunday: A Practical Guide for Worship Planning (Broadman Press, 1989)
Best Sermons 2 (Harper & Row, 1989)
Handbook of Contemporary Preaching (Broadman Press, 1993)
Admidst Babel, Speak the Truth (Smyth & Helwys, 1993)
Proclaiming the Baptist Vision: The Bible (Smyth & Helwys, 1994)
The University Through the Eyes of Faith (Light and Life, 1998)
The Minister's Manual (Jossey-Bass): *2000* (1999), *2002* (2001), *2003* (2002),
     2004 (2003) *2005* (2004), *2006* (2005), *2007* (2006)
Putting Women in Their Place (Smyth & Helwys, 2003)
Distinctively Baptist: Essays on Baptist History (Mercer University Press, 2005)
Gladly Learn, Gladly Teach: Living Out One's Calling in the 21ˢᵗ-Century Academy
     (Mercer University Press, 2005)
The Future of Baptist Higher Education (Baylor University Press, 2006)
Bound on Earth: A Festschrift for Edmon Lewin Rowell, Jr. (Mercer University Press, 2006)

PUBLICATIONS (PERIODICALS)

Theological Journals:
   Journal of Biblical Literature
   Review and Expositor
   Theological Education
   Faith and Mission
   Perspectives in Religious Studies
   Baptist Studies Bulletin
Religious Magazines:
   Covenant Companion
   The Christian Century
   The Christian Ministry
   Christianity Today
   The Pulpit
   Sermons of the Week
   Survey
   The Watchman-Examiner
   Pulpit Digest
   Christian Ethics Today
   Priscilla Papers
Denominational Publications:
   Baptist Faculty Paper
   Baptist Program
   Beam International
   Campus Minister
   Church Administration
   Contempo
   The Deacon
   The Southern Baptist Educator

Home Missions
Search
The Student
Sunday School Lesson Illustrator
The Window
Baptist State Papers
Baptists Today
Curriculum Materials:
    Baptist Sunday School Board "Life and Work" Curriculum
    Baptist Sunday School Board Uniform Lesson Series
Editorial Advisory Boards:
    Survey (1960-63)
    Review and Expositor (1964-68)
    Contributing Editor, *The Baptist Message* (1977-78)
    Best Sermons (Harper & Row, 1986-1989)
    Minister's Personal Library (Word, 1987-1989)

PUBLICATIONS (RECORDINGS)

"The Letters of John," Minister's Tape Plan (Broadman Press, 1970)
"Sermon on the Mount," Broadman Cassettes (Broadman Press, 1974)
"The Place of the Sunday School," Broadman Cassettes (Broadman Press, 1980)
"Effective Church Staff Relations," Broadman Cassettes (Broadman Press, 1981)
"Sunday School and Pastoral Priorities," Teach Tapes (International Center for
    Learning, 1981)
"The Centrality of Worship and Preaching," Timely Tapes (Scudder Communications
    Associates, 1983)
"Ministering in the Inner City," Broadman Cassettes (Broadman Press, 1984)

RECOGNITIONS/HONORS

Phi Eta Sigma, National Scholastic Fraternity, 1948
Omicron Delta Kappa, National Leadership Fraternity, 1951
Denominational Service Award, Samford University, 1974
Phi Kappa Phi, National Scholastic Fraternity, 1975
Liberty Bell Award, Shreveport Bar Association, 1984
Brotherhood and Humanitarian Award, Shreveport and Bossier City Chapter, NCCJ, 1987
Phi Alpha Theta, History Honor Society, 1988
Pi Gamma Mu, Social Sciences Honor Society, 1988
Lamplighter Award, Alabama League for Nursing, 1997
Charles D. Johnson Outstanding Educator Award, Association of Southern Baptist
    Colleges and Schools, 1999
Alumnus of the Year, Samford University, 2005
Spain-Hickman Distinguished Service Award, Rotary Club of Birmingham, 2006
Doctor of Letters honorary degree, Samford University, 2008
Rotary International District 6860 Vocational Service Award, 2009

BIOGRAPHICAL RECOGNITIONS

Contemporary Authors, vols. 17-18, 1967, p. 235; vols. 17-20, 1976, p. 362;
   new revision series, vol. 7, 1982, p. 239
Personalities of the South, 1972, p. 354; selected for 11th ed., 1981
Creative and Successful Personalities of the World, 1972, p. 337
International Scholars Directory, 1st ed., 1973, p. 115
Dictionary of International Biography, vol. 10, 1974, p. 883
Directory of American Scholars, 6th ed., 1974, vol. IV, p. 200
Outstanding Educators of America, 1975, p. 155
The Writers Directory, 1990-92, p. 201
Oxford's Who's Who, 1992
Who's Who in Religion, 4th ed., 1992-93
Who's Who in Biblical Studies and Archaeology, 2nd ed., 1992-93
Who's Who in the World, 12th ed., 1995
Who's Who in the South and Southwest, 33rd ed., 2006
Who's Who in American Education, 7th ed., 2006-07
Who's Who in America, 63rd ed., 2009

CPSIA information can be obtained at www.ICGtesting.com
Printed in the USA
BVOW05s0741281115

428727BV00026B/358/P